ULTIMATE cake

ULTIMATE
Cake

BARBARA MAHER
Photography by Dave King

DK Publishing, Inc.
www.dk.com

DK

A DK PUBLISHING BOOK
www.dk.com

Project Editor
Debbie Major

Editor
Kate Scott

Senior Editor
Carolyn Ryden

Art Editor
Jo Grey

Designer
Emy Manby

DTP Designer
Karen Ruane

Managing Editor
Susannah Marriott

Senior Managing Art Editor
Carole Ash

Recipe Consultant
Val Barrett

Home Economists
Janice Murfitt
Angela Kingsbury

Production Manager
Maryann Rogers

US Editor
Laaren Brown

First paperback edition, 1998
2 4 6 8 10 9 7 5 3

Published in the United States by DK Publishing, Inc.
95 Madison Avenue,
New York, NY 10016.

ISBN 0–7894–3760–0

A catalog record is available from the Library of Congress

Reproduced in Italy by GRB Editrice, Verona
Printed and bound in Singapore by Star Satndard Industries (Pte.) Ltd.

Contents

Introduction 6

A Gallery of Cakes 10

*A selection of some of the world's
most mouthwatering, tempting, and spectacular
cakes, shown whole and in slices to reveal
their delicious fillings.*

Baking Essentials 30

A full-color introduction to the key ingredients and equipment used in cake making, with a photographic guide to the basic techniques and principles of baking.

Icings, Fillings, & Decorations 138

Illustrated easy-to-follow instructions show how to achieve a professional finish with recipes for all the essential decorations, fillings, and toppings.

Recipes 58

More than 100 recipes for cakes to suit every occasion, with detailed step-by-step instructions and additional information on advance preparation, freezing, and storage.

Introduction

This is a book to savor. The cakes look good and taste even better. They are combinations of the best ingredients and the finest flavors – butter, eggs, flours, sugars, fresh and dried fruits, nuts, spices and extracts. It is almost a history book, for it brings together classic cake recipes from countries as far-flung as Italy, Sweden, and Japan, many with origins deep in the past. The different baking methods, influenced by travelers, immigrants, traders, and invaders, reflect the culture, folklore, and art of each nation's peoples throughout the centuries. And this diversity is still apparent today, for wherever one travels, one will find local specialties. As George Lang says in *The Cuisine of Hungary*, "Sacher torte is best in Vienna, Dobos is the finest in Budapest, cheesecake richest in New York," and recipes for all these cakes are included in this book.

The Origins of Cakes

The first cakes were made from simple ingredients as symbols of the mythical and magical superstitions of ancient religions. Early trade routes brought exotic spices from the Far East; nuts, perfumed flower waters, citrus fruit, dates, and figs from the Mideast; sugar cane from the Orient and South. During the Dark Ages in Europe these coveted ingredients were available only to monks and the wealthy aristocracy, who created cakes such as ginger and honey breads and cookies baked flat and hard. In time, an increase in trading brought about a complete transformation in the eating habits of the Western world. Arab traders and soldiers returning from the Crusades spread the use of spices and Mideastern-style recipes. In the principal trading towns of Middle Europe, guilds of bakers were formed, and by the late Middle Ages spices were being used extensively in wealthier households all over Europe, inspiring skillful and more imaginative baking. As nuts and sugar became popular, so did "marchepane" – marzipan baked in embossed and carved wooden molds depicting religious teachings.

A 17th-century cake mold

Cakes for Special Occasions

The most important and luxurious cakes were baked for religious
festivals. They combined local dairy produce and ingredients
that grew abundantly in the surrounding countryside with
expensive imported goods, such as nuts and spices.
Harvest-time cakes especially were cherished for their
keeping qualities through the winter months. Over
the years these cakes became traditional, and we
still bake them in the same way with identical
ingredients for our own celebrations.

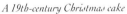

A 19th-century Christmas cake

The Emergence of a Café Society

An elaborate cuisine developed in the 16th- and 17th-century Italian
and French courts had, by the 18th century, become important in everyday
life, too. Small pastry shops opened that grew into "cafés," and Vienna,
with the lavish lifestyle of the Hapsburg court, a strong Turkish influence,
and a predilection for all things sweet, became the "Mother of Cafés." A
book of the time described a new confection as a "sumptuous cream-filled
picture, of eggs, sugar, butter, snow, and a little flour." These sophisticated
cakes as well as homey pastries, served with coffee and conversation,
became the rage. *Kaffeeklatsch* (café society) had arrived in Central Europe.

Scene in a 19th-century French pâtisserie

Afternoon tea in a Victorian household

Teatime

Afternoon tea appeared in late 19th-century Britain after the Duchess of Bedford entertained friends with an elegant repast between lunch and dinner. Plates of dainty sandwiches and cake stands laden with small, French-style fancy cakes were customary fare. Tea tables were laid with fine linen and costly silver or china tea services, and pretty napkins and silver forks were handed to each guest. As tea became less expensive it grew in popularity, and teatime became a ritual. In less wealthy homes, "high tea" was served to the whole family at around six o'clock. Cold dishes and homemade plain and fruited cakes were eaten with sweet, milky tea.

Baking Traditions in North America

In the 17th century, settlers from several European countries brought with them wholesome cooking and delicious traditional baking, rich in spices. These baked goods were sold at local markets, along with fresh produce. By the early 20th century, "bake sales" and competitions at country fairs had become popular; in cities, pastry chefs tried to outdo even the Viennese in their baking prowess. Cakes were now an essential feature of the North American table. Scandinavian settlers had brought with them a tradition for drinking coffee and eating Danish pastries. Combined with the fruity breakfast cakes, coffee and nut cakes, and doughnuts of Germanic Europe, "coffee klach" had found its way to the New World.

The Role of the Written Word

Cookbooks have also played a major part in spreading the
influence of different ethnic baking traditions. The writings in early
Arabic texts, the manuscripts of grand court kitchens, the scripts of humble
monks, guildsmen, master chefs, and even of the ordinary housewife have
crossed continents, been copied and translated into many languages.
The last 150 years have seen the swiftest and
greatest cultural exchanges.

It is from those early cookbooks that my own fascination
for baking has grown. For this book I have chosen a wide selection of
delicious recipes that are typical of their lands and traditional origins: from
simple butter cakes and light sponges filled with whipped cream
and brimming with ripe berries, to small crisp or chewy cookies to serve
with dessert, to grand confections suitable for the finest banquet.
You will also find wickedly rich chocolate marvels finished with truffles,
appealing children's party cakes decorated with candy, and
elegant, flower-topped wedding cakes. In all, there are more
than 100 recipes to tempt and indulge you. I do hope that they
will give you as much pleasure as they have given me.

Points to Remember for Successful Baking

Baking is a skill for which the maxim "Practice makes perfect"
really does hold true. In this book you will find many detailed, step-by-step
photographs of the basic techniques, plus practical tips designed to help you
achieve delicious and good-looking cakes. However, there are a few
essential rules that should always be followed carefully.

♦ *Choose a time when you can work without distraction or interruption.*

♦ *Be sure that you have all the ingredients required for any recipe before you start.*

♦ *Always use ingredients at room temperature.*

♦ *Measure out all the ingredients before you start mixing the cake.*

♦ *Follow the same units of measurement throughout a recipe; use either imperial or metric, but never a mixture of the two.*

♦ *The right baking pan is essential for perfect results. Be sure your pan is an appropriate size and shape for the recipe you have chosen before you begin to work.*

♦ *The oven should be turned on to preheat before preparation begins. This allows the oven to reach the recommended baking temperature before use.*

♦ *The correct oven temperature is crucial for baking success. For perfect accuracy, it is best to check the temperature with an oven thermometer placed in the center of the oven before baking the cake.*

♦ *The baking times given in each recipe can only be used as a guide because every oven varies. Check the cake approximately 5 minutes before the end of the baking time in the ways shown on page 50, then remove or leave in the oven.*

♦ ***Warning: Raw eggs can transmit salmonella. Avoid serving recipes containing raw eggs to the elderly, young children, and pregnant women.***

A Gallery of Cakes

This mouthwatering collection of delicious cakes, illustrated in full color, gives a tempting glimpse of the many exciting recipes you will find in the book. There are cakes for all occasions, and whether you prefer a multilayered creamy confection or a dark, rich chocolate sponge, a fresh fruit flan packed with juicy berries or an airy meringue, this inspiring guide will help you to make your choice.

Luxury Layer Cakes

Biscuit de Savoie (See page 65.)

Layer cakes were introduced to North America by 19th-century immigrants from central Europe, who set up their own Continental-style pâtisserie shops to sell these luxurious confections. Exquisite blends of flavors and textures make layer cakes as much a feast for the mouth as for the eyes.

"A torte – is one with a pleasing appearance inside and out."

Confectioner's description, early 20th century

Caramel slices rest on chocolate cream rosettes

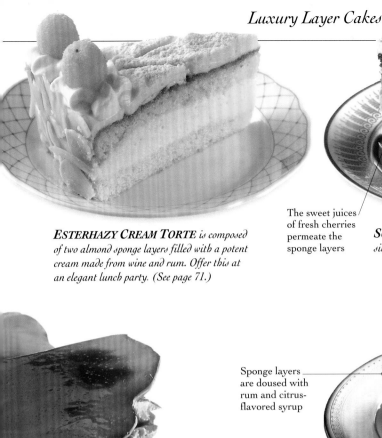

ESTERHAZY CREAM TORTE *is composed of two almond sponge layers filled with a potent cream made from wine and rum. Offer this at an elegant lunch party. (See page 71.)*

The sweet juices of fresh cherries permeate the sponge layers

SOUR CHERRY AND CHOCOLATE TORTE, *similar to Black Forest Kirschtorte. (See page 78.)*

Sponge layers are doused with rum and citrus-flavored syrup

RUM AND CITRUS TORTE *is typical of torten popular in 19th-century Austria and Germany. (See page 73.)*

DOBOS TORTA *(above and left) is traditionally a confection of thin sponge layers, sandwiched together with a rich chocolate buttercream and covered with a clear sheet of caramel glaze. Here the caramel is cut into triangles and set in a fan design. (See page 74.)*

HAZELNUT MACAROON CAKE *improves in flavor as it matures. (See page 75.)*

Chocolate Cakes

Chocolate Chestnut Roulade

Chocolatl, a rich yet bitter drink, was valued as highly as gold by Montezuma II, king of the Aztecs. Columbus took the cocoa bean back to Spain in 1502, where it was kept secret for more than 100 years. Eventually, in 1875, two Swiss chocolatiers created the first bar of milk chocolate, and so began the sweet revolution.

"From the fruit of the gods, the cocoa pod, comes the bean out of which cocoa powder and ten-pound chocolate bars are made."

Adrianne Marcus,
The Chocolate Bible (1979)

The ganache coating is made from chocolate and cream

Orange mousseline buttercream makes a delicious filling and topping

CARACAS *is a delicious, sophisticated chocolate sponge, baked in an elegantly shaped pan (see page 41) and covered with a rich chocolate ganache cream. (See page 84.)*

ORANGE AND CHOCOLATE LAYER CAKE *effectively blends the citric sharpness and tang of an orange filling with layers of delicately flavored chocolate cake. (See page 81.)*

A chestnut purée and dark rum filling complements the light sponge perfectly

CHOCOLATE CHESTNUT ROULADE *combines a moist sponge, full of chocolate and crunchy chopped nuts, and a filling of exquisite chestnut buttercream. (See page 82.)*

CHOCOLATE FORTISSIMO *is a wonderful Swiss specialty with hints of spices and coffee. The chocolate sponge is moistened with syrupy spirits, sandwiched with whipped cream and a smooth chocolate buttercream, then finished off with wickedly tempting truffles laced with Tia Maria. (See page 80.)*

SACHER TORTE *traditionally has no decoration other than its originator's name piped onto the highly glazed chocolate surface. I have done away with the writing and added a ring of chocolate leaves. (See page 83.)*

Moist almond and chocolate sponge

Tia Maria adds a heady kick to the chocolate truffles

Cheesecakes

Traditionally served at Pentecost, cheesecake is often considered to be of Jewish origin, but it may be Italian in ancestry – the ancient Romans are known to have eaten honey-flavored cheese in savory confections. Today cheesecakes are enriched with eggs and cream, enhanced with fruit, spices, or even chocolate.

"…the best way for these Cheesecakes is to make Coffynes in Patty-Pans, and fill them with the Meat near an Inch thick."

Richard Bradley, *The Country Housewife and Lady's Director* (1736)

Italian Easter Cake

ITALIAN EASTER CAKE *contains an unexpected filling of spiced ricotta cheese, cooked vermicelli pasta, and finely chopped candied citrus peel. (See page 133.)*

Raisins soaked in dark rum add texture and flavor to the cheese filling

GOLDEN BAKED CHEESECAKE *is rich and yet perfectly light in texture, full of flavor and studded with raisins, just the way it should be. (See page 111.)*

Apricot jam helps bind the crumb base, giving it a slight crispness

MANGO AND PASSION FRUIT CHEESECAKE*, light and wonderfully fluffy in texture, is perfumed with fresh orange and passion fruit juice. (See page 109.)*

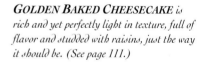

PASKHA *is reminiscent of delicious Italian cassata ice cream. A combination of nuts, peel, raisins, cream, and vanilla creates a rich and harmonious Russian Easter dessert. Use cream cheese instead of farmer cheese for a richer flavor. (See page 131.)*

PECHE MELBA CHEESECAKE *offers the sweet, delicate flavor of fresh peaches in a simple cheese filling. Serve with fresh raspberry sauce. (See page 110.)*

Slightly sharp, fresh raspberry sauce transforms this into a luxurious dessert

Slices of glacé fruit arranged like jewels on a Russian icon

Flans & Tarts

A flan or tart is a simple, crisp container or "coffyne," as it was once known, with a filling. The filling is the attraction, and whether it is eye-catching circles of fruit, glistening nutty mixtures, or tangy citrus custards oozing with baked aromatic juices, the results are sure to be irresistible.

Tarte Tatin

"A tart…is but a kind of dinner plate…which may be eaten."

E.S. Dallas,
Kettner's Book of the Table (1877)

Crème pâtissière prevents the fragrant fruit juices from soaking into the pastry

FRENCH FLAN WITH RED BERRIES
has both tart and sweet soft summer fruit packed tightly over crème pâtissière in a delicate pastry shell. (See page 91.)

GLAZED FRESH ORANGE FLAN
makes a rich and striking dessert. The texture of the fruit, glazed with a tangy marmalade-like syrup, contrasts well with the smooth, buttery orange filling and crisp, short pastry. (See page 92.)

Golden caramelized apples are baked under a crisp pastry crust

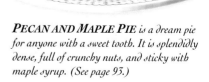

Shelled pecans arranged over the top in concentric circles

TARTE TATIN, *a warm upside-down tart made with caramelized apples, was created early in the 20th century by the Tatin sisters in France. (See page 95.)*

PECAN AND MAPLE PIE *is a dream pie for anyone with a sweet tooth. It is splendidly dense, full of crunchy nuts, and sticky with maple syrup. (See page 93.)*

Thinly sliced glazed
oranges create a
highly colorful,
shiny surface

Meringues

Simple meringues with cream

A pastry chef called Gasparini, who lived in Meiringen, Switzerland, was reputed to have created a composition of beaten egg whites and sugar in the 1720s. Affectionately known as "Meiringerli," these exceptionally light confections remain a specialty of the Bernese Oberland region but are popular everywhere.

"A jewel for the ladies... whose composition is as light and soft as whipped cream."

Antonin Carême, a famous 19th-century French chef

TORTA DI PIGNOLI *is made with lightly toasted pine nuts, which give flavor and crunch to the meringue layers. (See page 115.)*

Thick layer of chocolate ganache

JAPONAIS *is a classic French combination. The meringue disks contain lightly toasted, crunchy hazelnuts, and are sandwiched with luxurious chocolate ganache. (See page 117.)*

Decorated with fresh strawberries

SIMPLE MERINGUES *are sumptuous yet fragile creations, crisp on the outside and lightly aerated inside. Serve in pairs with whipped cream. (See page 112.)*

Meringue batons are arranged over the top

MOCHA TRANCHE, *with its flavored meringue and softly whipped cream, melts in the mouth, leaving the lingering warmth of chocolate and coffee. (See page 116.)*

SUMMER BERRY VACHERIN
makes a wonderful dessert for a special occasion. Meringue disks are layered with cream, flavored with liqueur and lightly crushed raspberries and strawberries. The spectacular confection is topped with a mouthwatering display of fresh summer fruit. (See page 114.)

Meringue is layered with raspberry and strawberry cream

Tart fruit contrasts with the sweet meringue

Fruit & Nut Cakes

Polish Coffee and Walnut Cake
(See page 103.)

Dried fruit and nuts are a classic combination. Chopped or ground nuts often replace butter and sometimes flour in a cake mixture because they are full of natural oils. They add subtle flavor and a distinctly rich and luxurious moistness to a cake, while fruit enhances the fragrance, deepens the texture, and improves the keeping quality of the cake.

" We were permitted only one piece of cake at tea-time, never two! To have two was considered greedy."

Michael Smith's Afternoon Tea
(1986)

Lemon glacé icing adds extra flavor

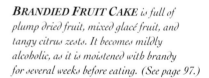

Some of the glacé fruit decoration should be served with each slice

SPICED HONEY CAKE *is a wonderful winter cake, rich and moist. It is lightly spiced with cinnamon, ginger, and cloves and then decorated with glacé icing and crystallized ginger. (See page 98.)*

BRANDIED FRUIT CAKE *is full of plump dried fruit, mixed glacé fruit, and tangy citrus zests. It becomes mildly alcoholic, as it is moistened with brandy for several weeks before eating. (See page 97.)*

Sliced almonds
dusted with
confectioners'
sugar

COCONUT LAYER CAKE, *a sweet and
fluffy cake, is an old-fashioned favorite.
The slightly sharp tang of strawberry jelly
complements the frosting of cream cheese and
the fresh coconut coating. (See page 106.)*

SPANISH ALMOND SPONGE, *with its
subtle taste of brandy or Grand Marnier and
orange zest, is good to serve at an afternoon
tea, filled with plenty of whipped cream and
crisp toasted almond slices. (See page 107.)*

CARROT AND HAZELNUT LOAF *is
flavored with grated carrot, chopped hazelnuts,
orange zest, and brown sugar, and topped with
a light cream cheese frosting. (See page 89.)*

Marzipan carrots
denote the key
ingredient

Pastries & Cookies

A selection of cookies

Whether described as "petits fours," "biscuits de pâtisserie," "friandises," cakes, or simply cookies, small edible temptations are offered in almost every country whenever richly roasted coffee and fine teas are served. They may be light and airy or chewy and crunchy, and they are always hard to resist.

"To make Short cakes… your paste will be very short, therefore ye must make your cakes very little…"

The Good Huswives Handmaid
(c. 1579)

A light dusting of confectioners' sugar adds to the appeal

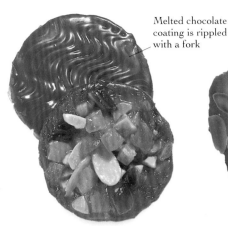

Melted chocolate
coating is rippled
with a fork

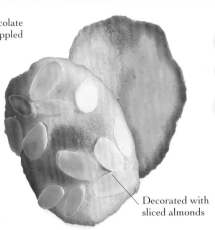

Decorated with
sliced almonds

FLORENTINES *are made from colorful glacé fruit and sliced almonds, baked in a toffeelike mixture and coated with melted chocolate. (See page 119.)*

TUILES *gain their name from the curved French roof tiles they resemble. Wafer-thin and very crisp, they are good served with ice cream desserts. (See page 120.)*

CHOCOLATE ECLAIRS *are traditional small French pastries, covered with semisweet chocolate and filled with a rich and creamy custardlike crème pâtissière. (See page 121.)*

FRUIT AND CREAM PUFFS *comprise crisp, golden domes of choux pastry filled to the brim with fresh soft fruit and lightly whipped cream. (See page 121.)*

A chocolate coating
makes these cookies
very tempting

Whipped cream
can be flavored
with liqueurs

BUTTER COOKIES *may be crisp to bite into, but they have a soft center. Traditionally the cookies are piped into rings, scrolls, or simple sticks and then dipped into melted semisweet chocolate. (See page 120.)*

SUGAR COOKIES *are sweet, buttery, and easy to make. Create different shapes by using decorative cutters, finish with a sprinkling of assorted colored sugars, then bake until crisp and golden. (See page 120.)*

Wedding Cakes

The rich and symbolic traditions of wedding cakes have developed over the centuries and remain with us today. Designed to be the centerpiece at a wedding feast and shared among the guests, the cakes are customarily multilayered and sumptuously decorated.

"I sing of maypoles, hock-carts, wassails, wakes, Of bridegrooms, brides and of the bridal cakes."

Robert Herrick, *Hesperides* (1648)

Croquembouche (See page 122.)

Buttercream icing piped in a basketweave pattern

Fresh flowers are pushed between the layers of cake

AUTUMN WEDDING CAKE
is made up of moist almond sponge layers flavored with orange zest and chocolate, sandwiched together and decorated with orange buttercream. The fresh flowers arranged at the base of each cake tier add the finishing decorative touches.
(See page 124.)

Sugar paste icing
gives the cake a
flawless finish

**TRADITIONAL
WEDDING CAKE** *has two
tiers of Baumkuchen and one of
Traditional Plum Cake covered
in marzipan and then smooth,
champagne-colored sugar paste.
The paste is decorated with
delicate sugar-frosted flowers.
(See page 126.)*

Tint the
sugar paste to
complement
the shade of
the flowers

Flowers are
arranged in
decorative
cascades

Children's Party Cakes

Ribbon and Candle Cake

Every child loves to have a special birthday cake, and here is a fantasia of ideas to mark the occasion. Designed to be fun to make as well as to look at, they also taste wonderful. Adapt the decorations to suit your own child's preferences and let your imagination run riot.

"He had a cake with icing on the top, and three candles, and his name in pink sugar…"

A. A. Milne, *Winnie the Pooh* (1926)

TEDDY BEAR CAKE *is ideal for young children with its light sponge and cheery decoration. Make a few extra presents for the party guests as take-home gifts. (See page 136.)*

RIBBON AND CANDLE CAKE, *made from a deliciously moist carrot sponge, is covered with soft cream cheese frosting and decorated with elegant candles and ribbons. (See page 137.)*

Brightly colored icing hides layers of plain and chocolate sponge

The number of balloons matches the age of the child

Chocolate thins overlapped to make roof tiles

PORCUPINE CAKE *has spikes of flaked chocolate and a sweet and fudgy chocolate cake center covered with rich chocolate icing. (See page 135.)*

The face is shaped from marzipan

Chocolate "quills" are pushed into the icing before it sets

Piped glacé icing window and door details

LITTLE HOUSES *are based on a simple layer-cake mixture, cut to shape and decorated in the style of traditional gingerbread. (See page 134.)*

Baking Essentials

Learn the basic skills required for baking from this clearly illustrated step-by-step guide. Packed full of useful hints and tips to ensure that your baking will be trouble-free, it teaches key techniques from separating an egg to checking a cake for doneness. Basic recipes are provided for the various types of pastry used in the book. There is also a photographic guide to the most useful kitchen tools and all the essential bakeware, plus a visual catalog of the best ingredients to select for your pantry.

Basic Ingredients

Keep a selection of these basic ingredients so that you can bake whenever you wish. The more unusual ones are available from health food stores. Your cakes and cookies will taste delicious and look most appetizing if you choose only the best-quality produce and the freshest dairy goods. Do not store any ingredients in large quantities as they soon deteriorate; it is better to keep smaller amounts and replace them more often.

Flours, Leaveners, & Thickening Agents

The baking qualities of flours vary according to their ability to form gluten when moistened. Gluten sets when heated, trapping air in the mixture. The gluten in all-purpose flour gives a soft texture; potato starch and cornstarch give more structure.

All-purpose and self-rising flour: *All-purpose flour is used on its own in whisked and rich fruit cakes and cookies, or together with a leavening agent. Self-rising flour already includes some baking powder.*

Rye flour: *A whole-grain brown flour that gives a rich color and a delicious nutty taste to cakes and tea loaves.*

Potato starch: *Made from boiled, sieved, and dried potatoes, this produces a delicately textured cake.*

Semolina flour: *Fine-grained, rich in protein and starch, this gives a good texture.*

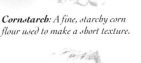

Cornstarch: *A fine, starchy corn flour used to make a short texture.*

Gelatin: *Gives a taste-free, firm set to soft cake fillings and cheesecakes.*

Matzo meal: *Crushed crumbs of unleavened crackers used in place of flour and as a thickener.*

Baking soda: *Acts as a leavening agent when combined with an acid such as lemon juice.*

Baking powder: *This reacts with moisture to produce carbon dioxide, which helps a cake to rise.*

Cream of tartar: *An acidic substance that stabilizes egg whites during beating.*

Sweeteners

Sugars and syrups affect the structure of a cake and improve its texture, color, and flavor. Store in airtight containers in a cool, dry place.

Superfine sugar: Best for making meringues and fruit desserts, because the fine crystals dissolve and blend quickly with other ingredients.

Golden syrup: Gives the finished cake a moist texture.

Honey: Used for centuries, a natural sweetener enhancing flavor and keeping quality of cakes.

Maple syrup: This natural sweetener has a strong, distinctive flavor.

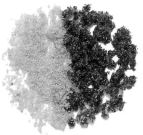

Confectioners' sugar: A fine, powdery sugar, ideal for icings and fillings. It must be sifted before use.

Granulated and colored sugars: Use granulated sugar for most cakes; colored for decorating.

Light and dark brown sugars: Raw cane sugars add moisture, color, and a caramel flavor to cakes.

Raw sugar: Unrefined with a low molasses content, this gives a good flavor to fruit and spice cakes.

Dairy Produce

Store dairy products in the refrigerator; butter may be frozen. If not fresh they will taint the baking. Fresh dairy products add a rich flavor to good baking.

Heavy cream: Contains a high percentage of fat, which allows it to be whipped firmly without separating.

Cream or farmer cheese: Full-fat cream cheese is richer and more creamy. Farmer cheese is lower in fat, drier, and slightly acidic.

Ricotta cheese: A slightly grainy, low-fat soft cheese with a sweet taste.

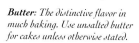

Eggs: Add flavor, color, and lightness to a cake. Use large eggs unless the recipe states otherwise. Always use at room temperature.

Milk: Good for moistening and loosening thick cake mixtures. Also gives a softer crust to choux pastry. Whole milk is most commonly used.

Sunflower or corn oil: For rich moisture in some fruit sponges and spiced cakes.

Butter: The distinctive flavor in much baking. Use unsalted butter for cakes unless otherwise stated.

Enriching Ingredients

Nuts, dried fruit, and spices were used extensively in the general cuisine of ancient times. Today they are important for enriching cakes and pastries. Buy in small amounts as spices soon lose their pungency and nuts become rancid and bitter after 3–4 months. Dried fruit also spoils with time. Store in airtight containers in a cool, dry place.

Nuts & Dried Fruit

Almonds: *Available whole, ground, or sliced, almonds are sweet to taste.*

Pistachios: *Their distinctive green kernels add color and flavor. Use unsalted ones and blanch before use.*

Pine nuts: *The soft, oily-textured seed of the stone pine has a strong flavor that is enhanced by baking.*

Hazelnuts: *Toast first to bring out their rich flavor.*

Walnuts: *Rich in oil and protein, with an unmistakable flavor.*

Pecans: *Flavorful and rich, these nuts are ideal for fruit cakes.*

Coconut: *Freshly grated, it gives moisture to a cake. Thinly pared shavings make a pretty decoration.*

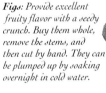

Figs: *Provide excellent fruity flavor with a seedy crunch. Buy them whole, remove the stems, and then cut by hand. They can be plumped up by soaking overnight in cold water.*

Golden raisins: *Produced from seedless green grapes. Add flavor by plumping in brandy before using.*

Dates: *A sun-dried fruit, these add moisture and sweet, rich flavor.*

Dark raisins: *Dried Muscatel grapes; seedless ones are the best.*

Dried cranberries: *Distinctive red berries with a piquant flavor.*

Dried apricots: *These soft, moist fruits may be plumped up before use.*

Flavorings & Spices

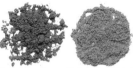
Instant coffee: An easy way to add rich coffee flavor.

Cocoa powder and chocolate drink powder: Crushed from the "chocolate liquor" of dried, roasted cocoa beans.

Dark rum: A strongly aromatic and richly flavored spirit distilled from sugar cane.

Brandy: Distilled from grapes, this spirit has a deep, mellow flavor.

Kirsch: A fiery eau de vie made from crushed fermented cherries.

Vanilla extract: Made by macerating crushed vanilla beans in alcohol.

Orange-flower water: Strongly perfumed distilled flower essence.

Tiny seeds lie inside the bean

Nutmeg: This dried kernel imparts a warm, richly aromatic flavor to many spiced cakes. Best used freshly grated.

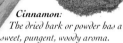

Vanilla bean and seeds: Add a sweet, mellow flavor. Make vanilla sugar by placing a bean in a jar of superfine sugar.

Whole nutmeg

Allspice: Also known as Jamaican pepper, this is sweet yet peppery.

Poppy seeds: Oily ripened seeds with a rich, nutty flavor.

Cinnamon: The dried bark or powder has a sweet, pungent, woody aroma.

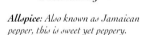

Cloves: Dried flower buds with a bitter, sharp flavor, these can be bought whole or in powder form.

Lemon and orange zest: Contain the essential flavoring oils.

Aniseed: Adds a distinctive, sweet, licorice-like flavor and can be bought as seed or a fine powder.

Buy pieces with smooth skin

Fresh ginger: Gives a sharp, hot, aromatic flavor.

Powdered ginger: A highly concentrated, spicy and hot flavor; be careful to use the correct measure.

Saffron: One of the most expensive spices, prized for its color and taste.

Decorating Ingredients

Even the simplest decorations enhance the texture and flavor of a cake. Fresh and glacé fruits have the greatest visual appeal, with their tempting bright and colorful appearance.

Chocolate and coffee finishes give a wonderful dark, rich look to cakes, and subtly colored and finely flavored icings offer luxurious stylishness with little effort.

Fresh Fruit

Raspberries: *Sweet, juicy ruby red berries; the richer their color, the riper and more delicious they are.*

Grapes: *Select seedless varieties to embellish dessert-style cakes.*

Apples: *Choose crisp, shiny fruit with a good color. Firm, flavorful apples are best for tarts and cakes as they stay whole during baking.*

Blueberries: *Deep purple-skinned berries with dark green flesh, these are sweet yet tart and acidic, and blend well with other soft fruit.*

Strawberries: *These have a sweet, refreshing flavor. Choose firm, undamaged fruit with an even color and bright green stems.*

Oranges and lemons: *Strongly aromatic citrus fruit with a sweet acidic flavor. They add color and help neutralize any cloying sweetness in baking.*

Glacé Fruit

Glacé citron peel and clementines: *Buy good quality fruit that is soft-textured and not too sweet. Rinse off the excess sugar or syrup before using, if desired.*

Mixed chopped peel: *Precut orange and lemon peel is available.*

Angelica: *The crystallized stem of a large garden herb.*

Natural and red glacé cherries: *Wash in warm water before baking to remove the sugary surface, then dry thoroughly on kitchen towels.*

Glacé pineapple: *Cut the whole circular slices to the size you require.*

Crystallized ginger: *Has a strong, sharp tang, so use sparingly.*

Preserves

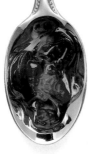

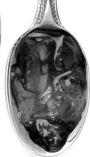

Chestnut purée: *The canned, unsweetened purée is good for use in cake fillings.*

Seedless raspberry jam: *Ideal as a sweet, distinctive filling in light sponge cakes.*

Red currant jelly: *Sharp, tangy, and very fruity.*

Apricot jam: *Adds a sharp, fruity flavor and helps bond icings to a cake's surface.*

Marmalade: *Use this citrus fruit preserve as a glaze for a glacé fruit decoration.*

Strawberry jelly: *Crystal clear with a tart sweetness.*

Chocolate

Chocolate coffee beans: *Roasted coffee beans covered in chocolate.*

Chocolate buttons: *Small chocolate disks are ideal for children's cakes.*

Chocolate shapes make easy decorations

Chocolate: *Semisweet chocolate containing 50–70% cocoa solids has the richest and best flavor for baking. Milk and white chocolate have less flavor but are good for decoration.*

Chocolate thins: *Slim squares of chocolate can be made by hand or bought from a candy store. They make good decorations for cakes, whole, halved, or cut into triangles.*

Chocolate sticks: *Narrow strips of flavored milk or semisweet chocolate are useful for decorating both children's party cakes and more sophisticated chocolate cakes.*

Colorings

Be careful when using any food colorings as they are all very concentrated. Dip the tip of a fine skewer into the coloring, adding very gradually until the right shade is achieved. Remember that colors darken with time.

Red paste

Green liquid

Yellow liquid

Essential Tools & Baking Equipment

Here is a basic selection of the most useful equipment to have in the kitchen when you are baking cakes. A few more unusual items are also shown as they do make certain tasks much easier. When buying tools, always choose the best quality available: they last longer, are more reliable, and produce the best results. For successful baking, a complete set of measuring cups and spoons is essential, since ingredients must be measured carefully.

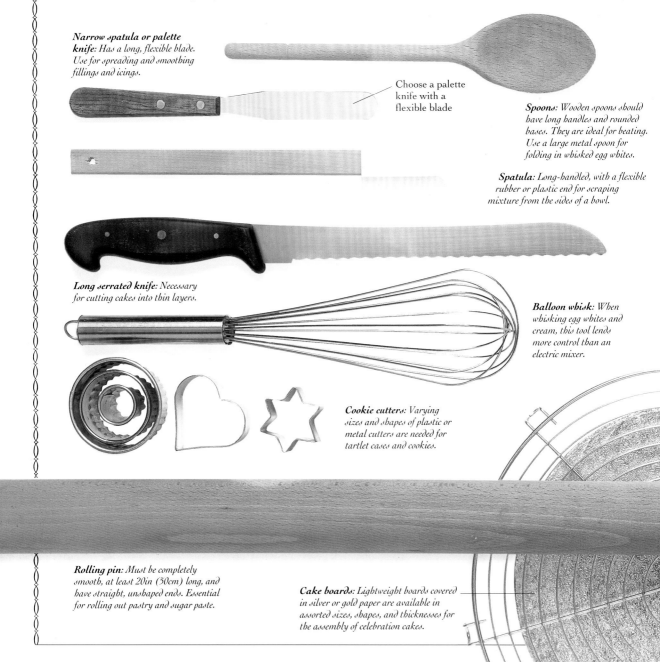

Narrow spatula or palette knife: *Has a long, flexible blade. Use for spreading and smoothing fillings and icings.*

Choose a palette knife with a flexible blade

Spoons: *Wooden spoons should have long handles and rounded bases. They are ideal for beating. Use a large metal spoon for folding in whisked egg whites.*

Spatula: *Long-handled, with a flexible rubber or plastic end for scraping mixture from the sides of a bowl.*

Long serrated knife: *Necessary for cutting cakes into thin layers.*

Balloon whisk: *When whisking egg whites and cream, this tool lends more control than an electric mixer.*

Cookie cutters: *Varying sizes and shapes of plastic or metal cutters are needed for tartlet cases and cookies.*

Rolling pin: *Must be completely smooth, at least 20in (50cm) long, and have straight, unshaped ends. Essential for rolling out pastry and sugar paste.*

Cake boards: *Lightweight boards covered in silver or gold paper are available in assorted sizes, shapes, and thicknesses for the assembly of celebration cakes.*

Glass mixing bowls: The best bowls are made of strong, heatproof glass and have smooth, rounded bases.

Grater: This should have one coarse and one fine grating face, and one coarse and one fine zesting face. Good for chocolate, fine citrus zest, and fresh nutmeg.

Measuring cup: A clear, heatproof cup showing both metric and standard measurements is best.

Sieve: Use metal sieves for dry ingredients and plastic for fruit purées.

Candy thermometer: Essential when boiling sugar syrups.

A range of piping nozzles for cake decorating

Nylon pastry bag: Available in various sizes, these bags give best results and can be washed and reused.

Large piping nozzles: Designed for piping cream, meringue, and choux pastry.

Small piping nozzles: Perfect for finely detailed chocolate and iced decorations.

Pastry brush: Use for applying glazes, brushing pastry, and pans.

Citrus zester: Removes zest in long, thin strands.

Pastry wheel: Shaped to cut pastry decoratively.

Measuring spoons: Accurate spoon measurements are possible with these. Must always be level unless otherwise stated.

Vegetable peeler: A swivel-bladed steel peeler is ideal for apples and pears and removing strips of lemon zest. You can also use it for making chocolate curls.

Wire racks: Allow air to circulate beneath cooling cakes, dispersing any steam and preventing cakes from getting soggy and heavy.

Bakeware

Choose good-quality, heavyweight baking pans that conduct heat efficiently and evenly. Matte-finished metal pans or sturdy nonstick pans are best. Inexpensive pans made from thin, lightweight metal wear out quickly and conduct heat badly, causing cakes to burn and cook unevenly. Also avoid cheap, shiny pans and glass bakeware. Wash, rinse, and dry all bakeware thoroughly in a warm oven before and after use.

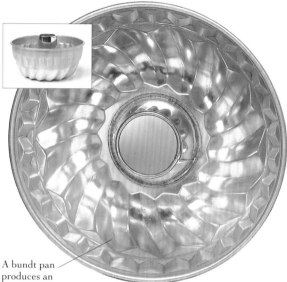

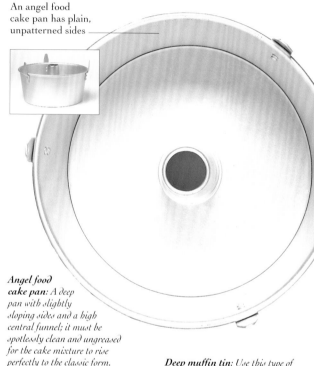

An angel food cake pan has plain, unpatterned sides

A bundt pan produces an attractive shaped cake

Angel food cake pan: *A deep pan with slightly sloping sides and a high central funnel; it must be spotlessly clean and ungreased for the cake mixture to rise perfectly to the classic form.*

Deep, round pan: *Loose- or fixed-bottomed deep-sided pans available in various sizes are good for rich, heavily fruited cakes that require longer baking. Line with paper before using.*

Bundt pan: *This deep, elaborately patterned, sloping-sided pan has a central funnel that helps the cake to bake through evenly and quickly.*

Deep muffin tin: *Use this type of pan for making small cheesecakes. Choose one with a nonstick finish.*

Jelly roll pan: Ideal for roulades.

Flat baking sheet: Use for cookies, meringues, and choux pastry.

Layer cake pans: Shallow, straight-sided pans with fixed or loose bottoms. Good for baking sponge cake layers.

Tart pan: This is loose-bottomed with fluted sides and available in different shapes, sizes and depths. Choose one with deeper sides if there is lots of filling.

Springform pan: A loose-bottomed pan with its sides held together by a spring clip, making it easier to remove the cake.

Loaf pan: A deep, rectangular pan with rounded corners is perfect for making quick breads. Available in different sizes. Line before using.

A Balmoral pan has decorative ribbed sides

Deep, square pan: With a loose or fixed bottom, this is for cakes that need longer baking. Shallower pans are better for sponge cakes and sheet cakes.

Balmoral pan: Long, semi-circular pan for rich tea breads.

Preparing Cake Pans

The type and size of pan is crucial to a cake's success. Always use the size stated in the recipe and check by measuring across the top, from one inside wall to the other. Depth is also important: too shallow and the mixture will overflow; too deep and the cake will not rise properly. All pans require some form of preparation, depending on the style of cake.

Greasing & Lining

Preparing a cake pan helps stop the cake from sticking. Odd-shaped pans should be greased twice with butter, then dusted with flour. Other pans can be lined with baking parchment, which has a nonstick finish, or waxed paper, which needs to be brushed with more butter. Rich fruit cakes also benefit from a paper collar around the pan to prevent them from overbrowning and drying out.

--- **HANDY TIPS** ---

◆ Make sure that all your bakeware is spotlessly clean and dry before you start.

◆ Greasing before lining keeps the paper in place.

LINING A ROUND OR LARGE SQUARE PAN

1 Brush the inside of the pan evenly with melted butter. Cut one strip of paper to fit around the sides, overlapping slightly, making sure it is 2in (5cm) wider than the depth of the pan.

2 Fold in one long edge of the paper by 1in (2.5cm) and crease well. Unfold and then make angled cuts at 1in (2.5cm) intervals along this edge, up to the folded line.

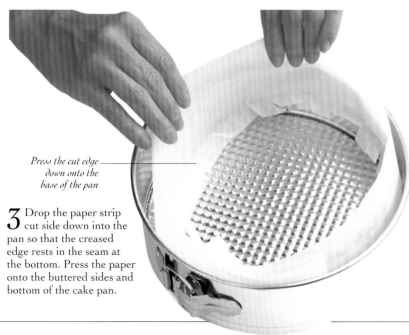

Press the cut edge down onto the base of the pan

3 Drop the paper strip cut side down into the pan so that the creased edge rests in the seam at the bottom. Press the paper onto the buttered sides and bottom of the cake pan.

4 Place the bottom of the pan on another piece of paper. Draw a faint pencil line neatly around the bottom. Cut out the paper circle just inside the pencil line so that the paper disk will fit snugly into the bottom of the cake pan.

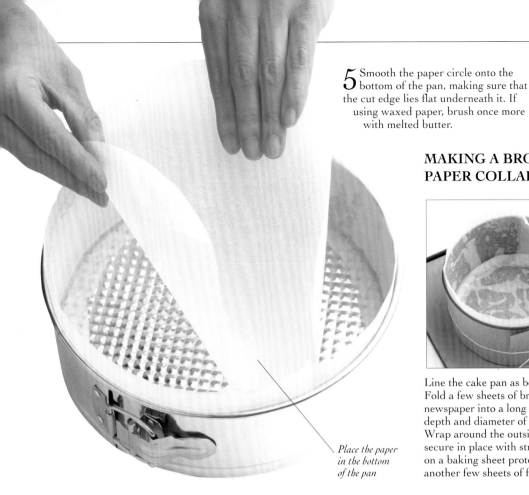

5 Smooth the paper circle onto the bottom of the pan, making sure that the cut edge lies flat underneath it. If using waxed paper, brush once more with melted butter.

Place the paper in the bottom of the pan

MAKING A BROWN PAPER COLLAR

Line the cake pan as before with paper. Fold a few sheets of brown paper or newspaper into a long strip to match the depth and diameter of the cake pan. Wrap around the outside of the pan and secure in place with string. Rest the pan on a baking sheet protected with another few sheets of folded paper.

LINING A SMALL SQUARE OR LOAF PAN

1 Place the pan in the middle of a sheet of paper, large enough to extend up the sides and beyond by 1in (2.5cm). Draw around the bottom. Crease along these lines. From the longer sides, cut along the creases up to the marked lines.

2 Grease the bottom and sides of the pan. Fold up the sides of the rectangle and drop into the pan, tucking the flaps behind the longer sides. Press onto the bottom and sides, securing the paper at the corners with more butter.

DUSTING WITH FLOUR

Grease the bottom and sides of the pan and place in the refrigerator for a few minutes. Repeat once more. Spoon in a little flour and tilt the pan until the sides are evenly coated. Turn over and tap the bottom to remove any excess.

General Baking Skills

Once baking begins, it is essential to avoid any interruption so that the steps of preparation may follow each other in quick succession. All the ingredients should be fully prepared – measured, sifted, ground, melted, or grated – before you start to combine them. Cake pans should also be greased and lined and the oven preheated to the correct temperature.

SIFTING FLOUR

Shake the flour twice through a fine sieve held high over a bowl. This fills it with air and improves the cake's texture. Sift once more with any additional dry ingredients so they are evenly mixed.

SEPARATING EGGS

Carefully crack the shell on the edge of a clean bowl. Break the egg and, without splitting the yolk, quickly pour it from one half shell to the other, letting the white fall into the bowl below.

ZESTING CITRUS FRUIT

Rub the skin of a scrubbed or unwaxed lemon over the finest side of a grater, without removing any of the bitter white pith underneath. A citrus zester (see page 39) removes longer strands.

MELTING CHOCOLATE

Melt the chocolate until smooth and glossy

Break the chocolate into pieces and place in a small heatproof bowl. Rest over a saucepan of barely simmering water and leave for about 5 minutes, stirring occasionally, until melted.

TOASTING HAZELNUTS

1 Toast on a baking sheet at 350°F/ 180°C for 15 minutes, until lightly browned and with flaking skins.

2 Pour the hot nuts onto a cloth. Fold the cloth over them and rub gently to remove the skins. Cool before using.

BLANCHING PISTACHIOS

Drop shelled, unsalted pistachios into boiling water and let soak for 2–3 minutes. Drain, slide off the skins, and let dry before using.

TOASTING BREAD CRUMBS

Spread out slices of stale crustless bread on a wire rack. Bake at 275°F/140°C for 45 minutes–1 hour until dry, crisp, and golden. Cool and break into small pieces. Either grind to a powder in a food processor or place in a plastic bag and crush with a rolling pin. Sift through a fine-mesh sieve to remove the coarser crumbs.

WHIPPING CREAM

Pour heavy cream into a bowl and whip with a balloon whisk or an electric mixer until it has formed soft peaks that turn over at the ends. For piping, whip the cream until it forms slightly stiffer peaks, but be careful not to overwhip, especially in warm conditions, or the cream will curdle and separate. Chantilly cream is whipped cream sweetened with sugar and flavored with brandy or vanilla. It can be used as a filling or decoration.

Soft peaks with the cream turning over at the end

———— *HANDY TIPS* ————

• *Always use cream straight from the refrigerator or it may separate.*

• *Chill your bowl and beaters to very cold before you whip and you will get better volume.*

DISSOLVING GELATIN

Gelatin must be softened in cold liquid and then dissolved before using. Cool the dissolved gelatin before blending into a mixture or it will form strings. Use 1 teaspoon of gelatin powder to 1 tablespoon of liquid.

———— *HANDY TIPS* ————

• *Always add the gelatin to the liquid or lumps will form and it will not dissolve properly.*

• *Do not overheat the gelatin or it will lose its setting properties.*

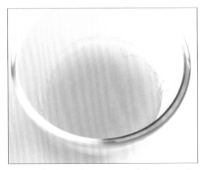

1 Put the liquid into a small heatproof bowl. Sprinkle over the gelatin and let soften for 5 minutes.

2 Set the bowl in a small pan of barely simmering water. Leave until clear and dissolved. Cool before using.

Basic Methods

Creaming and whisking are the two main methods for making cakes. The ingredients must always be handled with care and should be at room temperature before you start.

Incorporate as much air as possible while beating or whisking: an electric mixer will make this a lot easier. Then lightly fold in the additional ingredients by hand.

CREAMED CAKE MIXTURES

These cakes have a moist, slightly dense texture. Vigorous creaming together of the butter, sugar, and eggs incorporates the air that is essential to produce a good cake.

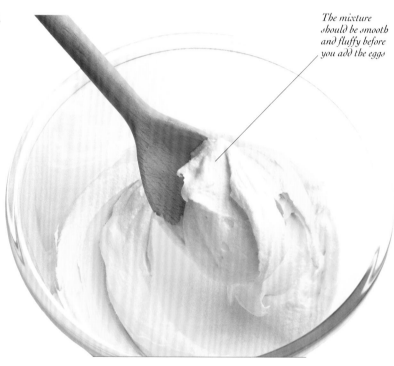

The mixture should be smooth and fluffy before you add the eggs

1 Beat the butter in a mixing bowl for 1–2 minutes, until soft and creamy. Add the sugar and beat vigorously for 3–5 minutes, until it is pale and fluffy and has doubled in volume (right).

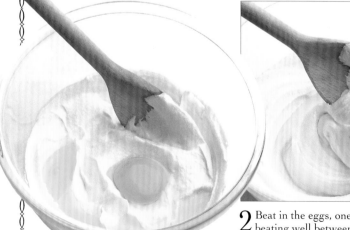

2 Beat in the eggs, one at a time (left), beating well between each addition. The mixture will initially loosen, then thicken when ready for the next egg.

3 Spoon the already sifted flour into the sieve or sifter. Hold the sieve a little above the bowl and sift once more over the creamed mixture.

5 The finished cake mixture should be smooth, thick, and creamy and drop reluctantly off the spoon.

4 Gently fold in the flour with a large metal spoon, using a cutting and folding action. Do not stir or beat the mixture or the added air will be lost.

HANDY TIPS

◆ *Use a generous-sized bowl so that there is enough room in which to beat the mixture.*

◆ *A separated mixture holds less air; adding a little flour with the last egg or two prevents this.*

WHISKING EGG WHITES

If whisking egg whites to fold into a cake mixture, do not whisk them too stiffly: they will not blend in evenly, making the cake look blotchy.

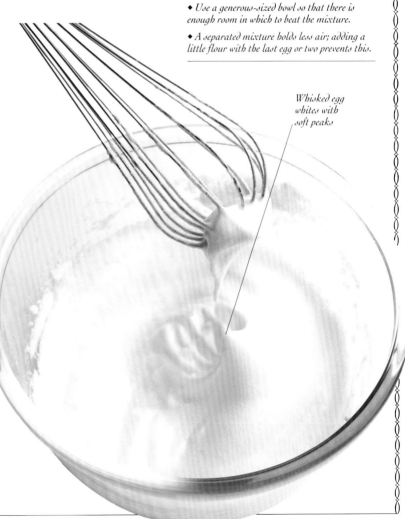

Whisked egg whites with soft peaks

1 Place the egg whites in a spotlessly clean bowl. Using a balloon whisk or an electric mixer, whisk the egg whites slowly, until foamy.

2 Start to beat the egg whites faster, until they increase in volume and stand in peaks that are still soft enough for the ends to turn over.

WHISKED CAKE MIXTURES

Whisked cakes have a very light, delicate, open texture. Bake them immediately: if left to stand the mixture will collapse.

The mixture should leave a trail on the surface

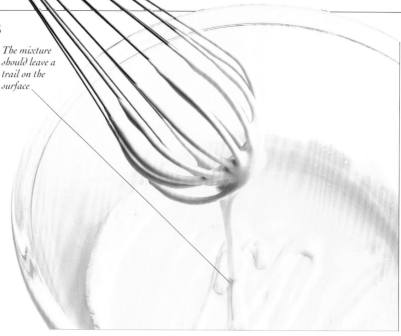

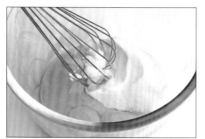

1 Whisk the egg yolks and sugar in a large bowl to the ribbon stage; the mixture will be pale, thick, and doubled in volume. If drizzled over the surface it holds its shape for 4–5 seconds (right).

2 Whisk the egg whites into soft peaks. Stir 2 large spoonfuls into the egg yolk mixture to loosen the texture slightly. Sift over and gently fold in the flour using a large metal spoon.

3 Trickle the melted butter around the edge of the mixture, without adding the milky sediment, and gently fold it in.

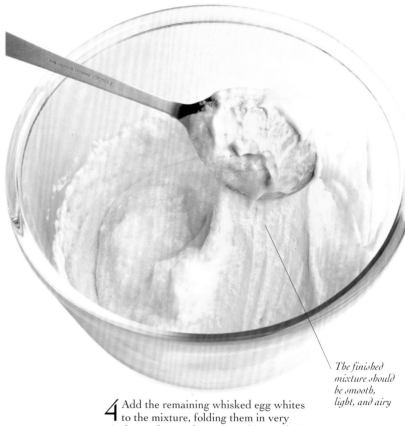

The finished mixture should be smooth, light, and airy

4 Add the remaining whisked egg whites to the mixture, folding them in very gently, until everything is evenly mixed. Be careful not to overwork the mixture.

MAKING SIMPLE MERINGUES

The whisking of egg whites traps air; adding cream of tartar and sugar helps stabilize the mixture and prevents it from separating.

1 Whisk the egg whites until foamy. Add the cream of tartar and whisk into soft peaks. Gradually whisk in half the sugar, 1 tablespoon at a time.

2 Either fold in the rest of the sugar, a few spoonfuls at a time, using a metal spoon, or to form a stiffer meringue for piping, continue to whisk it in gradually.

Whisk the meringue until dense and stiff peaks form

SHAPING MERINGUES

For individual meringues, push large spoonfuls of mixture onto parchment-lined baking sheets.

MAKING MERINGUE DISKS

1 Spoon the meringue mixture into a nylon pastry bag fitted with a ½ in (1cm) plain nozzle.

2 Mark circles on a lined baking sheet. Pipe from the center outward, in a continuous spiral, to just inside the line.

Pipe just within the marked circle

3 To check that a meringue is done, lift it off the paper, turn it over, and gently tap the underside. It should sound hollow and be crisp and dry to the touch.

Cooking & Turning Out Cakes

Cakes generally cook best in the center of a preheated oven. Check that the racks are in position and that the temperature is correct before placing the cake inside. Avoid opening the door once the cake has started to bake until at least three quarters of the cooking time has passed; a sudden draft will cause the unstable structure to collapse.

CHECKING FOR DONENESS

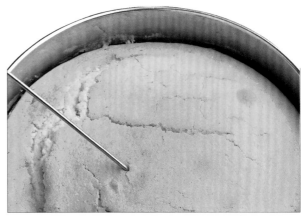

A cooked sponge cake should be well risen, golden, and just starting to shrink away from the sides of the pan. It should also spring back when you press the top softly with a finger.

All types of cakes may be tested by inserting a fine metal skewer into the center. The skewer should come out clean. If any mixture clings to it, bake for another 5 minutes.

TURNING OUT

1 Let the cake rest in the pan for a few minutes. If unlined, run a butter knife or narow spatula around the inside edge of the pan to loosen the sides of the cake.

2 To take out of the pan, release the clip and remove the sides of a springform pan. Stand loose-bottomed pans on an upturned bowl and allow the sides to slip down. Cakes in solid-bottomed pans can be inverted straight onto a wire rack (see step 3).

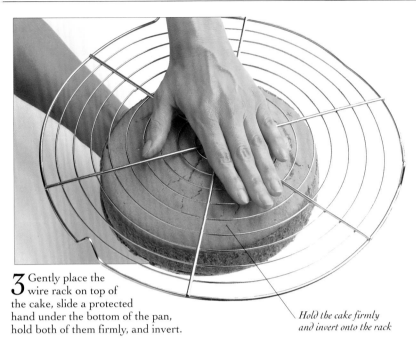

3 Gently place the wire rack on top of the cake, slide a protected hand under the bottom of the pan, hold both of them firmly, and invert.

Hold the cake firmly and invert onto the rack

4 Slide a narow spatula between the cake and the bottom of the pan and remove. Carefully peel off the lining paper without tearing the delicate structure of the cake, and let cool.

HANDY TIPS

♦ *If more than one cake is being baked at a time, they may need rotating in the oven and may take a little longer to cook.*

♦ *For a layer cake that needs a smooth, flat top, cool the cake with the bottom up.*

TURNING OUT A ROULADE

For undecorated roulades, remove the sponge from the oven and turn out onto waxed paper or baking parchment sprinkled with sugar.

Turn out using a dish towel

1 Quickly invert the hot roulade onto the prepared paper and carefully lift off the pan.

2 Pull out the edges of the paper from underneath the roulade. Release the paper at one corner and slowly peel back, taking care not to tear the delicate sponge, especially at the edges. The cake is now ready to be filled and rolled.

HANDY TIPS

♦ *Turning the roulade out onto sugar stops it from sticking to the paper.*

♦ *Roulades that are turned out while hot must be rolled up immediately or they will crack.*

Layering, Rolling, & Storing Cakes

The plainest cakes taste exquisitely rich when layered with special fillings. Some of the more elaborately layered cakes do take a little effort to complete, so allow plenty of time for assembling them and then chill for at least 4–5 hours to allow the layers to settle and the flavors to blend. Correctly storing cakes will enable you to eat them at their best.

LAYERING

1 Place the cake on a firm, level surface. Rest a hand lightly on top of the cake to hold it steady. Slice the cake horizontally through the center with a sharp, long-bladed, serrated knife.

2 Starting with the top layer, carefully separate the cake layers by sliding the bottom of a tart pan between them. When each layer is fully supported, lift off and set to one side until needed.

3 For additional flavor, lightly sprinkle each cake layer with a little liqueur or flavored sugar syrup (see page 153). Let it soak in well before spreading with the filling.

4 Starting with the bottom cake layer, spread each one evenly with a portion of the filling, to within ¼in (5mm) of the edge. Cover with the next layer and press down gently.

Spread the filling
in an even layer

5 Neatly even the edges of the buttercream layers before finishing.

HANDY TIP

♦ *Simple sponge cakes are best filled and eaten on the day they are made. Some of the more lavishly filled cakes taste better if they are left to mature for a day or two before serving.*

FILLING A ROULADE

1 Using a large narrow spatula, carefully spread the filling in an even layer over the surface of the warm, turned out roulade, taking it to within ½in (1cm) of the edge.

2 Neatly trim about ½in (1cm) off each of the edges. Using the back of a large knife, score a shallow, straight line along one short end of the sponge, about 1in (2.5cm) in from the edge.

3 With the scored end facing you, lift up the edge of the paper and use it to help support and guide the cake as you roll it up. Gently roll the roulade over so that the seam lies underneath.

4 Cut about ½in (1cm) off each end of the roulade to give a neat finish. Let cool on a wire rack. Carefully lift up the roulade using two large narrow spatulas and transfer to a serving plate, seam side down.

— *HANDY TIP* —

♦ *Roulades that are to be filled with whipped cream or buttercream need to be covered with waxed paper, then a slightly damp dish towel and left to cool before turning out, filling, and rolling. This prevents them from drying out.*

A roulade looks attractive with a contrasting filling

CUTTING CAKES

Cutting the first slice of a cake is always difficult. Using a long, sharp, pointed knife, lightly insert the tip into the center of the cake. Holding it at right angles to the cake, gently cut down through the layers with a slight sawing action. Determine the size of the slice, then make a second cut in the same way. Slide the blade of the knife as far under the slice as you can and gently start to ease it out. If it won't come away easily, then carefully recut either side of the slice. Subsequent slices will be easier to remove.

SERVING CAKES

As time and trouble have been taken to prepare a cake, a little effort in its presentation is worthwhile. Choose a serving plate that matches the cake's character – for example, elegant, delicate china for an elaborate, multilayered extravaganza or a plain, country-style plate for a more simple cake. Present the slice with some ceremony on a matching small cake plate, with a cake fork on the side and a napkin at hand if you wish. The added effort and attention to such detail will be appreciated.

STORING & FREEZING

Cakes must be well wrapped to prevent them from drying out. A layer cake filled with cream or chocolate is best kept refrigerated in a large, airtight container; one with a flat bottom and domed lid is ideal. Other layer cakes must be stored in a cool place. Wrap undecorated cakes in waxed paper, then foil and store in an airtight container. To freeze, wrap the cake in waxed paper or foil and place in a freezer bag. Remove the air, then seal, label, and date. Defrost, still wrapped, in a cool place or in the refrigerator.

Pastry Making

Pâte brisée, or shortcrust pastry, is very slightly sweetened with sugar. *Pâte sucrée*, or sweet shortcrust pastry, is a sweeter, shorter pastry. It can either be pressed into the pan or rolled out between sheets of waxed paper. *Pâte sablée*, or sweet pie pastry, is very short and crisp, and ideal for all sweet pies and tarts.

One quantity of each recipe below will line a 9½in (24cm) tart pan.

PATE BRISEE

INGREDIENTS

1¼ cups (180g) all-purpose flour, sifted
pinch of salt
7 tbsp (100g) chilled butter
2 tbsp granulated sugar
1 egg yolk, lightly beaten
1–2 tbsp ice water

1 Sift the flour once more, together with the salt, into a large mixing bowl or onto a clean work surface. Make a well in the center.

2 Cut the chilled butter into pieces and add to the flour. Lightly rub the butter and the flour together with the tips of your fingers, lifting the mixture and letting it fall back down, until you have a fine, crumblike mixture.

Lightly fork the sugar through the mixture

3 Add the sugar to the bowl and stir in with a fork, making sure it is evenly distributed throughout the mixture.

4 Mix the egg yolk with the water until well blended. Drizzle over the mixture, stirring continuously with a small, round-bladed knife.

6 Gently bring the small lumps of pastry together using the heel of the hand until they form a rough ball. The quicker you do this the better.

5 Working swiftly yet lightly, continue to stir everything together until the mixture starts to stick together in little lumps.

The dough should form a neat ball

7 Knead briefly on a floured work surface until smooth. Cover with plastic wrap and chill for at least 1 hour.

--- **HANDY TIPS** ---

◆ *Pastry will keep in the refrigerator for 4–5 days, tightly covered in plastic wrap.*

◆ *Chilling the pastry before rolling out prevents it from shrinking during baking.*

VARIATION WITH PROCESSOR

Sift the flour, salt, and sugar into the bowl of the food processor. Add the chilled butter pieces and blend in short bursts for 10–15 seconds, or until it has formed a fine, crumblike mixture. Do not allow the crumbs to form into large lumps as this will overwork the mixture. Mix the egg yolk with a teaspoon of water (less water is needed for this method). With the motor running, quickly pour the liquid into the bowl and blend for a few seconds until the mixture has formed a compact ball. Turn the pastry out on a lightly floured surface, knead briefly and gently until smooth, then cover tightly with plastic wrap and chill for at least 1 hour before using.

PATE SUCREE

INGREDIENTS

scant 1¼ cups (170g) all-purpose flour
pinch of salt
7 tbsp (100g) chilled butter
¼ cup (60g) granulated sugar
1 tsp finely grated lemon zest
1 egg yolk, lightly beaten
1–2 tbsp ice water

Make the pastry following the main recipe for Pâte Brisée, adding the grated lemon zest with the sugar. Chill well before using – overnight if possible or for at least 1 hour. Allow the pastry to come back to room temperature, then knead briefly before using.

PATE SABLEE

INGREDIENTS

1¼ cups (180g) all-purpose flour, sifted
6 tbsp (90g) chilled butter
½ cup (60g) confectioners' sugar, sifted
1 tsp finely grated lemon zest
1 egg yolk, lightly beaten
1–2 tbsp ice water

Make the pastry following the main recipe for Pâte Brisée, adding the grated lemon zest with the sifted confectioners' sugar. Chill the pastry well before using – overnight if possible or for at least 1 hour. Allow the pastry to come back to room temperature, then knead briefly before using.

MAKING A PASTRY CASE

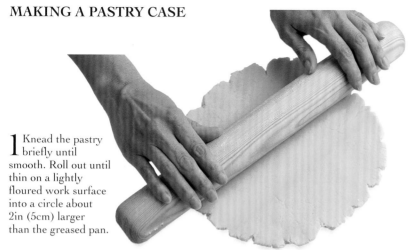

1 Knead the pastry briefly until smooth. Roll out until thin on a lightly floured work surface into a circle about 2in (5cm) larger than the greased pan.

2 Lightly rest the rolling pin over the center of the pastry. Fold one side of the pastry over the pin, carefully lift the pastry across the pan, and unroll.

3 Using floured fingers, carefully ease the pastry into the bottom and up the sides of the pan. Make sure that the pastry is firmly pressed into the seam where the bottom and sides meet.

4 Ease the excess pastry out over the edge of the tart pan. Run a rolling pin over the top of the pan to remove it. Patch any breaks in the pastry with the trimmings, sealing with a little water.

5 Firmly press the pastry onto the sides of the tart pan, whether fluted or plain, using your index finger. Chill for at least 1 hour to help prevent shrinkage during baking.

6 To bake with pie weights, prick the base of the pastry case all over with a fork. Line neatly with a single sheet of waxed paper or a double thickness of aluminum foil.

7 Fill the paper-lined case with a thin layer of dried beans, rice, or ceramic pie weights. This will prevent the bottom from rising and keep the sides in place. Bake according to the recipe.

Pastry case ready to bake with dried beans

— *HANDY TIPS* —

♦ *Make sure the pastry is at room temperature before rolling it out.*

♦ *If the baked case is to contain a moist filling, brush the hot pastry with egg white to seal.*

CHOUX PASTRY

Choux pastry gets its name from the French phrase *pâte à chaud*, meaning heated pastry, as it is cooked twice. The paste puffs up to three times its size when done.

INGREDIENTS

1 cup (125g) unbleached all-purpose flour
pinch of salt
2 tsp granulated sugar
7 tbsp (100g) butter
1 cup (250ml) water
4 eggs, lightly beaten

1 Sift the flour, salt, and sugar onto creased waxed paper. Melt the butter in the water in a large, heavy-bottomed pan. Bring to a rolling boil.

2 Take off the heat, add the flour, return to the heat, and beat rapidly into a smooth, glossy paste that rolls cleanly off the sides and base of the pan.

3 Allow the paste to cool for about 5 minutes. Then start to beat in the eggs, a little at a time.

4 Continue adding the eggs until the mixture is smooth and glossy – you will probably need only about 3½ eggs. Reserve the rest for glazing. Spoon into a pastry bag fitted with a plain nozzle.

The mixture should fall reluctantly from the spoon

5 Pipe small mounds of paste onto the prepared baking sheet. Glaze with the rest of the egg. Bake for 15–20 minutes. Pierce the bases with a skewer and bake 5 minutes longer. Let cool on a wire rack.

HANDY TIPS

- *Run a lightly greased baking sheet under cold water and leave slightly wet.*
- *Pipe the puffs far apart on the baking sheet.*

3

Recipes

A classic collection of recipes dating back to the 16th century is provided in this international repertoire of cakes, ranging from the Kastella of Japan, to Hungarian Poppy Seed and Chocolate Torte, to a Pumpkin Pie from North America – all complete with introductory material. The selection includes traditional cakes for festivals and weddings, as well as exciting ideas for children's birthday cakes. There is something here to please everyone.

Butter Cakes

Simple butter cakes are very easy to make. They are based on a combination of the key cake ingredients: butter, sugar, eggs, and flour, in varying proportions. These recipes are for plain, tasty cakes that are satisfyingly rich with a buttery texture and excellent flavor, ideal for serving with a cup of coffee in the afternoon or after dinner. Although they are not elaborate, the addition of special ingredients such as chocolate, fresh fruit, spices, or nuts, together with a coating of sweet glacé icing, readily transforms them into memorable treats.

Pound Cake

In her 1747 book, The Art of Cookery Made Plain and Easy, *Hannah Glasse explained how to "Make a Pound Cake" using a pound of flour, a pound of butter, a pound of sugar, eight eggs and "a great wooden Spoon." Today we no longer have to make such large quantities or rely on the spoon – using a machine makes much lighter work.*

INGREDIENTS

1 cup (125g) all-purpose flour, sifted
¼ cup (125g) potato starch
1 tsp baking powder
1 cup (250g) butter
1 cup plus 2 tbsp (250g) granulated sugar
seeds from ¼ of a vanilla bean
4 large eggs
1 tsp finely grated lemon zest
1 tbsp milk
confectioners' sugar to decorate

1 Sift the all-purpose flour, potato starch, and baking powder together. Set aside. Beat the butter, sugar, and vanilla seeds together until pale and fluffy. Beat in the eggs, one at a time, adding a little of the flour if the mixture begins to separate. Beat in the lemon zest.

2 Gradually beat in the flour until everything is evenly mixed. Stir in the milk. Spoon the mixture into the prepared pan and bake in the preheated oven for 1 hour, or until a fine skewer inserted into the cake comes out clean.

3 Remove the cake from the oven, ease away from the sides of the pan, and let rest for 10 minutes. Invert onto a wire rack and let cool. Transfer to a plate and dust with confectioners' sugar.

VARIATIONS

Fresh Fruit Pound Cake
Make the basic mixture, omitting the milk. Pit and roughly chop ½lb (250g) apricots, apples, plums, or peaches into ½in (1cm) pieces. Stir in 1 tablespoon lemon juice and fold the fruit into the basic mixture. Bake for 1¼ hours. Decorate with 1 quantity lemon glacé icing (see page 152) and fine lemon shreds (see page 149) once cold.

Chocolate Marble Pound Cake
Make the basic mixture, omitting the milk. Put half into another bowl and stir in 2 tablespoons cocoa powder blended with 2 tablespoons dark rum and 2½oz (75g) melted semisweet chocolate (see page 44). Drop alternating spoonfuls of each mixture into the prepared pan and bake for 1 hour. Decorate with 1 quantity chocolate glacé icing (see page 152) once cold.

Mixed Spice Pound Cake
Sift 1 teaspoon ground cinnamon and ½ teaspoon grated nutmeg with the flour. Fold into the basic mixture with ¼ cup (60g) chopped toasted hazelnuts (see page 45). Bake for 1 hour. Decorate with granulated sugar, cinnamon, and chopped hazelnuts once cold.

Oven temperature
350°F/180°C

Baking time
1 hour; 1¼ hours for the fresh fruit cakes

Cake pan
5 cup (1.5 liter) bundt pan, greased twice with melted butter and floured

Makes
12–16 slices

Storage
Fruit cakes keep for 2–3 days; others for 5–6 days

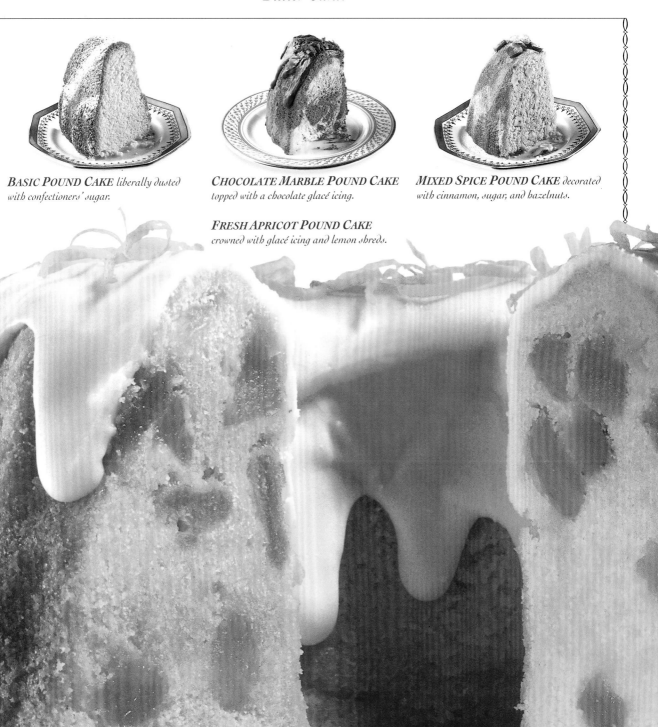

BASIC POUND CAKE *liberally dusted with confectioners' sugar.*

CHOCOLATE MARBLE POUND CAKE *topped with a chocolate glacé icing.*

MIXED SPICE POUND CAKE *decorated with cinnamon, sugar, and hazelnuts.*

FRESH APRICOT POUND CAKE *crowned with glacé icing and lemon shreds.*

Swedish Butter Ring

This treat may be eaten as is or spread with butter. It should be eaten the day it is made, or better still while it is slightly warm from the oven.

INGREDIENTS

For the filling

½ cup (90g) glacé cherries, chopped

½ cup (90g) candied orange and lemon peel, finely chopped

1 tsp finely grated orange zest

3 tbsp fine-shred marmalade

For the pastry

1½ cups plus 2 tbsp (250g) self-rising flour

½ cup (125g) butter, cut into small pieces

⅓ cup (60g) semolina flour

¼ cup (60g) granulated sugar

1 egg

2 tbsp milk

For the decoration

1 tbsp milk for brushing

1 tbsp crystal sugar

1 For the filling, mix together the cherries, candied peel, and orange zest. Set aside.

2 For the pastry, sift the flour into a bowl, add the butter, and cut into a fine crumblike mixture. Stir in the semolina and sugar. Mix the egg with the milk. Stir into the dry mixture until everything begins to stick together, then knead briefly.

3 Roll out the pastry on a lightly floured surface into a 12x9½in (30x24cm) rectangle. Spread over the marmalade to within 2in (5cm) of each long edge. Sprinkle with the filling.

4 Starting with one long edge, roll up the pastry and then twist it into a ring, pinching the edges together at the seam to seal. Carefully lift onto the prepared baking sheet and pinch together any large cracks with your fingers. Put a greased 2in (5cm) round metal cookie cutter into the center of the ring.

5 For the decoration, brush the ring with the milk and sprinkle with the sugar. Bake in the preheated oven for 25–30 minutes, or until golden. Remove from the oven, carefully transfer to a wire rack, and let cool slightly. Serve warm, spread lightly with butter if you wish.

 Oven temperature
400°F/200°C

 Baking time
25–30 minutes

 Cake pan
Flat baking sheet, greased

 Makes
8 slices

 Storage
Best eaten the day it is made

Hungarian Coffee Cake with Sour Cream

Traditionally served with steaming hot cups of strong coffee, this delicious cake contains layers of cinnamon and chopped nuts.

INGREDIENTS

For the cake

¾ cup (180g) butter

½ cup (125g) granulated sugar

1 tbsp vanilla sugar

2 eggs

⅔ cup (150ml) sour cream

2 cups plus 2 tbsp (275g) all-purpose flour

2 tsp baking powder

½ tsp baking soda

pinch of salt

For the filling

scant ½ cup (100g) granulated sugar

2 tsp ground cinnamon

1 cup (100g) pecans, chopped

1 For the cake, beat the butter, granulated sugar, and vanilla sugar together until pale and fluffy. Beat in the eggs, one at a time, followed by the sour cream.

2 Sift the flour, baking powder, baking soda, and salt together. Add to the butter mixture and beat together well.

3 For the filling, mix the sugar, cinnamon, and nuts together with a fork. Spoon one third of the cake mixture into the prepared pan and sprinkle over one third of the filling. Repeat twice more, ending with filling.

4 Bake in the preheated oven for 50 minutes–1 hour. Remove from the oven and let rest for 5 minutes. Remove from the pan and cool on a wire rack.

 Oven temperature
350°F/180°C

 Baking time
50 minutes–1 hour

 Cake pan
8in (20cm) springform pan, greased and floured

 Makes
12 slices

 Storage
Keeps for 2 days

 Freezing
Freezes for 1–2 months

Lemon Syrup Butter Cake

This is one of those "a little now, a little later" cakes that no one can resist. It has a sharp, fruity tang and is easy to make.

INGREDIENTS

For the cake

½ cup (125g) butter

½ cup (125g) granulated sugar

1 tbsp finely grated lemon zest

1 tbsp finely grated orange zest

2 large eggs

1 cup (125g) cake flour, sifted

1 tsp baking powder

2 tbsp warm water

For the syrup

2 tbsp lemon juice

2 tbsp orange juice

scant ½ cup (100g) granulated sugar

1 For the cake, beat the butter, granulated sugar, lemon zest, and orange zest together in a large bowl until pale and fluffy. Beat in the eggs, one at a time, adding a little of the flour with the second egg if the mixture begins to separate.

2 Sift the remaining flour and baking powder together. Beat into the butter mixture, followed by the water.

3 Spoon the mixture into the prepared pan and bake in the preheated oven for 35–45 minutes, or until a skewer comes out clean.

4 For the syrup, put the lemon juice, orange juice, and sugar in a small, heavy-bottomed pan and heat gently until the sugar has dissolved. Keep warm.

5 Remove the cake from the oven and prick the top all over with a fine skewer. Spoon over half the syrup and let stand for 2–3 minutes. Invert onto a wire rack and peel off the lining paper. Prick the base of the cake, pour over the rest of the syrup, and let cool.

 Oven temperature
350°F/180°C

 Baking time
35–45 minutes

 Cake pan
6½ x 4½ x 2¼in (16.5x11x5.5cm) loaf pan, greased and lined

 Makes
12 slices

 Storage
Keeps for 1 week

Freezing
Freezes for 1–2 months

Blitzkuchen

Similar to a pound cake mixture but baked in a shallow pan, these buttery slices are topped with a delicious cinnamon-spiced almond crumble.

INGREDIENTS

For the cake

2 eggs

½ cup (125g) granulated sugar

1 cup (125g) all-purpose flour, sifted

½ cup (125g) butter, melted and cooled

1 tsp finely grated lemon zest

For the topping

¾ cup (100g) all-purpose flour, sifted

2 tsp ground cinnamon

¼ cup (60g) granulated sugar

½ cup (75g) ground almonds

5 tbsp (75g) unsalted butter, melted and cooled

1 For the cake, beat the eggs and sugar together until pale and frothy. Beat in the flour, followed by the melted butter and lemon zest, until everything is evenly mixed. Pour the mixture into the prepared pan, making sure the corners are filled and even.

2 For the topping, sift the flour and cinnamon together into another bowl. Stir in the granulated sugar and ground almonds. Gradually pour in the melted butter, mixing all the time with a fork, until you have a coarse, crumblike mixture.

3 Sprinkle the crumb mixture evenly over the surface of the cake mixture. Bake in the preheated oven for about 25–30 minutes, or until golden. Remove from the oven, cut into slices, and let cool in the pan on a wire rack. Remove from the pan once cold.

VARIATION
For a different topping, mix ½ cup (75g) sliced almonds with 1 teaspoon ground cinnamon and 2 tablespoons granulated sugar. Sprinkle evenly over the surface of the cake mixture and bake as for the main recipe.

 Oven temperature
375°F/190°C

Baking time
25–30 minutes

Cake pan
13x9x2in (33x23x5cm) shallow, rectangular pan, greased and lined

 Makes
15 slices

 Storage
Keeps for 3–4 days

Sponge Cakes

Sponge *biskuit* appeared in European cookery manuscripts as early as the mid-16th century, sometimes softly textured but often like a hard cookie. The egg mixture was usually heated, then tediously whipped to cool it down. Today, the cold method, which uses separated eggs, takes much less time, and the sponge cake remains a favorite in any cook's repertoire. Its light and airy structure gives a delicious background for soft fruit and whipped cream, for aromatic spices, nutty textures, and fruity spirits, and of course, for chocolate.

Whipped cream laced with kirsch adds to the delicious contrast of flavors

Fresh strawberries and raspberries make a tempting decoration

Biscuit de Savoie

INGREDIENTS

For the cake

⅔ cup (60g) all-purpose flour
½ cup (60g) potato starch
2 cups (180g) confectioners' sugar, sifted
5 eggs, separated
pinch of salt
2 tsp lemon juice
½ tsp orange-flower water or 1 tsp dark rum

For the filling and decoration

6 tbsp (90ml) kirsch-flavored syrup (see page 155)
1 pint (500ml) fresh strawberries
½ pint (250ml) fresh raspberries
4 tbsp granulated sugar
1¼ cups (450ml) heavy cream
1 tbsp kirsch
strawberry leaves and confectioners' sugar

In France, Germany, and Austria, biscuit is the usual name for light sponge cakes. Potato starch and eggs are the key ingredients for producing this light, airy mixture. It is especially suitable for layer and rolled cakes that require a firmer and slightly drier sponge.

1 For the cake, sift the flour and potato starch together three times. Set aside.

2 Reserve 3 tablespoons of the confectioners' sugar. Whisk the remaining sugar and the egg yolks together to the ribbon stage (see page 48).

3 In another bowl, whisk the egg whites and salt into soft peaks (see page 47). Sift over the reserved sugar and whisk until they form slightly stiffer peaks. Fold in the lemon juice.

4 Stir 2 large spoonfuls of the egg white into the egg yolk mixture to loosen the texture. Gently fold in the flour and the orange-flower water or rum. Carefully fold in the remaining egg whites, taking care not to deflate the whites.

5 Pour the mixture into the prepared pan and bake in the center of the preheated oven for 35–40 minutes, or until a skewer comes out clean.

6 Remove from the oven and let rest in the pan for 5–10 minutes. Turn out onto a wire rack and let cool. Peel off the lining paper once cold.

TO FINISH THE CAKE

1 Slice the cake horizontally into three layers. Sprinkle the bottom two layers with the kirsch-flavored syrup. Place the bottom layer on a serving plate, syrup side up.

2 Set aside a few of the best strawberries and raspberries for the decoration. Remove the stems from the remaining strawberries and cut them into quarters. Mix the raspberries with 1 tablespoon of the granulated sugar. Whip the remaining sugar, the cream, and the kirsch into stiff peaks.

3 Carefully spoon the quartered strawberries evenly over the bottom cake layer, to within ½ in (1cm) of the edge. Spoon over one third of the whipped cream and spread evenly over the fruit. Cover with the second syrup-soaked cake layer, syrup side up. Spoon over the raspberries and spread out, followed by another third of the cream. Cover with the top cake layer and press it down lightly so that the fruit becomes embedded in the cream.

4 For the decoration, spread the remaining cream evenly over the top of the cake, using a metal spatula. Arrange the reserved whole berries in the center, and decorate with the leaves. Dust with confectioners' sugar just before serving.

 Oven temperature
350°F/180°C

 Baking time
35–40 minutes

 Cake pan
8½ in (22cm) springform pan, greased and lined

 Makes
8–10 slices

 Storage
Keeps for 2–3 days in the refrigerator

 Freezing
Freezes for 1 month, undecorated

 Step ahead
Make the kirsch-flavored syrup

BISCUIT DE SAVOIE combines delicate sponge, kirsch-flavored cream, and juicy summer berries.

Victoria Sandwich Cake

A traditional recipe in the British baking repertoire, and similar to Pound Cake (see page 60) in proportions, this simple, foolproof recipe is quick and easy to make.

INGREDIENTS

1 cup (250g) butter, softened

1 cup (250g) granulated sugar

4 eggs

1½ cups (250g) self-rising flour

1–2 tbsp milk

4 tbsp seedless raspberry jam

granulated sugar to decorate

1 In a large bowl, beat the butter and granulated sugar together until pale and fluffy. Beat in the eggs, one at a time, adding a little of the flour if the mixture begins to separate.

2 Sift the remaining flour over the surface of the mixture and fold it in, followed by a little milk to give the mixture a soft dropping consistency.

3 Divide the mixture in half and spread it evenly into the prepared pans. Bake in the preheated oven for 25 minutes, or until pale golden and soft and springy to the touch.

4 Remove from the oven and invert onto a wire rack. Let cool. Carefully remove the lining paper and spread the bottom of one cake with the raspberry jam. Cover with the second cake layer, transfer to a plate, and sprinkle the top with granulated sugar to decorate.

 Oven temperature
350°F/180°C

 Baking time
25 minutes

 Cake pans
Two 8in (20cm) round pans, greased and lined

 Makes
6–8 slices

 Storage
Keeps for 2–3 days

 Freezing
Freezes for 3 months, undecorated

Chiffon Cake

This is a close relation of angel food cake – a moist, light cake composed mostly of egg whites and sugar. For a Chiffon Cake, egg yolks and oil are included to give it a firmer structure and to allow it to take on flavors successfully, as in the Chocolate Mocha variation.

INGREDIENTS

1½ cups (180g) cake flour

2 tsp baking powder

1¼ cups (250g) granulated sugar

½ tsp salt

⅓ cup (75ml) corn or sunflower oil

5 egg yolks

½ cup (125ml) cold water

1 tsp vanilla extract

1 tsp finely grated lemon zest

5 egg whites

½ tsp cream of tartar

confectioners' sugar to decorate

1 Sift the flour, baking powder, sugar, and salt together twice and then once more into a bowl. Make a well in the center and add the oil, egg yolks, water, vanilla extract, and lemon zest. Gradually whisk the dry ingredients into the liquid until the mixture is smooth and shiny.

2 In another bowl, whisk the egg whites and cream of tartar into soft peaks (see page 47). Gently fold into the main mixture a third at a time, taking care not to deflate the whites.

Pour into the prepared pan and bake in the preheated oven for 45–50 minutes, or until a skewer comes out clean.

3 Remove from the oven and invert onto a wire rack. Leave in the pan until cold. Carefully run a round-bladed knife around the sides of the pan and the central tube and turn out. Let rest for 1 day before serving. Dust with confectioners' sugar to decorate.

VARIATIONS
Almond Chiffon Cake
Fold ¾ cup (100g) ground almonds into the finished cake mixture. Bake as before.
Chocolate Mocha Chiffon Cake
Melt 3oz (90g) semisweet chocolate with 2 teaspoons instant coffee dissolved in 1 tablespoon boiling water (see page 44). Sift 1½ teaspoons ground cinnamon with the flour, baking powder, sugar, and salt. Add the oil, egg yolks, water, and vanilla. Omit the lemon zest. Beat together well and stir in the chocolate mixture. Fold in the whisked egg whites and bake.

 Oven temperature
325°F/160°C

 Baking time
45–50 minutes

 Cake pan
9½in (24cm) angel food cake pan, spotlessly clean

 Makes
12 slices

 Storage
Let rest for 1 day before serving; keeps for 2–3 days

 Freezing
Freezes for 1–2 months

Rich Genoise Sponge

When butter is added to a fat-free sponge it is known as a Genoise. The addition of butter improves the flavor of the cake and also enhances its keeping properties. Genoise Sponge also freezes well. Use unsalted butter, which has a sweet flavor, never margarine. This is a richer version of a traditional Genoise, which usually has half this amount of butter.

INGREDIENTS

For the cake

½ cup (125g) unsalted butter

½ cup (125g) granulated sugar

4 large eggs, separated

1 tsp finely grated lemon zest

¾ cup (100g) all-purpose flour, sifted

For the filling and decoration

½ quantity lemon mousseline buttercream (see page 150)

confectioners' sugar

1 For the cake, melt the butter in a small pan over low heat. Remove from the heat. Let cool.

2 Set aside 2 tablespoons of the granulated sugar. Whisk the remaining sugar and the egg yolks together to the ribbon stage (see page 48), then whisk in the lemon zest.

3 In another bowl, whisk the egg whites into soft peaks (see page 47). Sprinkle over the reserved sugar and whisk to form slightly stiffer peaks.

4 Carefully fold 2 large spoonfuls of the egg whites into the egg yolk mixture to loosen the texture. Gently fold in the flour, followed by the melted butter, taking care not to add any of the milky liquid that collects in the bottom of the pan. Gently fold in the remaining egg whites, taking care not to deflate them.

5 Pour the mixture into the prepared pan and bake in the preheated oven for about 45–50 minutes, or until golden and a skewer inserted into the cake comes out clean.

6 Remove the cake from the oven and let rest in the pan for 5 minutes. Turn out onto a wire rack, peel off the lining paper, and let cool.

7 Cut the cake horizontally in half. Sandwich together with the lemon buttercream. Transfer the cake to a serving plate and dust lightly with confectioners' sugar to decorate.

  Oven temperature
350°F/180°C

  Baking time
45–50 minutes

 Cake pan
8½in (22cm) springform pan, greased, floured, and lined

 Makes
8 slices

 Storage
Keeps for 1 week

Freezing
Freezes for 2–3 months, undecorated

Step ahead
Make the lemon mousseline buttercream

Japanese Kastella

Although it may be the most popular cake in Japan today, Kastella originated in Portuguese Madeira, and is reputed to have been brought to the southern Japanese island of Kyusha in the 16th century. Traditionally, it is offered with a cup of green tea. As presentation and style are very important in Japanese culture, serve this cake in small slices on elegant plates, perhaps with whole, long-stemmed strawberries set alongside.

INGREDIENTS

6 egg yolks

scant ½ cup (100g) granulated sugar

2 tsp honey

pinch of salt

5 tbsp (75ml) condensed milk

⅔ cup (90g) all-purpose flour, sifted

4 egg whites

confectioners' sugar to decorate

1 Whisk the egg yolks and sugar together to the ribbon stage (see page 48). Whisk in the honey, salt, and condensed milk.

2 Stir the flour into the egg yolk mixture. In another bowl, whisk the egg whites into soft peaks (see page 47). Stir 2 large spoonfuls of the whisked egg whites into the egg yolk mixture to loosen the texture. Carefully fold in the remaining egg whites, taking care not to deflate them.

3 Pour the mixture into the prepared pan and bake in the preheated oven for 45 minutes, or until richly golden and a skewer inserted into the cake comes out clean.

4 Remove from the oven and let rest in the pan for about 5 minutes. Invert onto a wire rack, carefully peel off the lining paper, and let cool.

5 To decorate, dust the top of the cake with confectioners' sugar just before serving.

Oven temperature
325°F/160°C

  Baking time
45 minutes

 Cake pan
8½in (22cm) springform pan, greased and lined

 Makes
16 slices

 Storage
Keeps for 2–3 days

 Freezing
Freezes for 2–3 months

Biscuit Roulade with Rice Flour

Rice flour has an almost nutty flavor and aroma. It makes a light and fluffy sponge that holds its shape when cool. A jam filling complements it well. Offer this cake to people who don't eat wheat and they will feel very spoiled.

INGREDIENTS

For the cake

6 eggs, separated

6 tbsp (90g) granulated sugar

½ cup plus 1 tbsp (75g) rice flour

For the filling and decoration

6–8 tbsp apricot or raspberry jam, sieved

granulated sugar

1 For the cake, whisk the egg yolks and sugar together to the ribbon stage (see page 48).

2 In another bowl, whisk the egg whites into soft peaks (see page 47). Gently fold the flour, then the egg whites, into the egg yolk mixture, taking care not to deflate the whites.

3 Pour the mixture into the prepared pan. Lightly level the surface, making sure the corners are filled. Bake in the center of the preheated oven for 6–8 minutes, or until soft and springy to the touch.

4 Remove the cake from the oven and invert onto a sheet of waxed paper sprinkled with granulated sugar. Peel off the lining paper.

5 Spread the surface of the sponge with the jam and then, starting with one short edge, roll up (see step 2 opposite). Let cool on a wire rack. Transfer to a plate and sprinkle with granulated sugar.

 Oven temperature
400°F/200°C

 Baking time
6–8 minutes

 Cake pan
15x10x¾in
(36x25x2cm)
jellyroll pan,
greased and lined

 Makes
12–14 slices

 Storage
Keeps for 2 days

 Freezing
Freezes for
1–2 months

Piskóta with Walnuts

This sponge cake was brought into the Hungarian court of King Matthias in the late 15th century, after he married Princess Beatrix, the daughter of the king of Naples. This Piskóta is made as a roulade and flavored with walnuts.

INGREDIENTS

For the cake

4 eggs, separated

½ cup plus 1 tbsp (75g) granulated sugar

1 tsp instant coffee

2 tsp dark rum

¼ cup (90g) walnut pieces, finely chopped

For the filling

1¼ cups (300ml) heavy cream

1 tbsp dark rum

2 tbsp granulated sugar

For the decoration

7oz (200g) semisweet chocolate

walnut pieces, very finely chopped

1 For the cake, whisk the egg yolks and sugar together to the ribbon stage (see page 48). Dissolve the instant coffee in the rum and whisk into the egg yolk mixture.

2 In another bowl, whisk the egg whites into soft peaks (see page 47). Carefully fold the walnut pieces into the egg yolk mixture, followed by the egg whites, taking care not to deflate the whites.

3 Pour the mixture into the prepared pan. Lightly level the surface, making sure the corners are filled. Bake in the preheated oven for about 15–20 minutes, or until lightly browned and soft and springy to the touch.

4 Remove from the oven and invert onto a sheet of waxed paper sprinkled with granulated sugar. Cover with a slightly damp dish towel and let cool.

5 For the filling, whip the cream, dark rum, and granulated sugar into soft peaks. Remove the cloth from the roulade and peel off the lining paper. Spread the cream over the roulade, then roll up (see steps 1 and 2 opposite).

6 For the decoration, melt the chocolate (see page 44), then spread it evenly over the roulade with a narrow spatula. Let cool slightly, then swirl gently with a fork (see step 3 opposite). Sprinkle over the walnut pieces and let set before serving.

 Oven temperature
350°F/180°C

 Baking time
15–20 minutes

 Cake pan
15x10x¾ in
(36x25x2cm)
jelly roll pan,
greased and lined

 Makes
12 slices

 Storage
Keeps for
2–3 days

Filling and Rolling the Piskóta

1 Remove the dish towel and peel off the lining paper. Spread the rum-flavored cream over the Piskóta in an even layer to within 1in (2.5cm) of the edge.

2 Starting with one short edge, roll up the sponge using the paper to support and guide it. Place, seam side down, on a wire rack set over a large baking sheet or plate.

3 Pour the melted chocolate over the Piskóta and spread evenly over the cake's surface. Leave for a few minutes to cool slightly and then make swirls in the chocolate with a fork.

DECORATING THE PISKOTA

Sprinkle the chocolate surface of the cake with the walnut pieces and let set. Carefully transfer to a serving plate.

A delightful nutty sponge, filled with fresh cream

Luxury Layer Cakes

In the 19th century, cakes were influenced by the French chef Antonin Carême, who, guided by his love of sculpture and architecture, created highly elaborate masterpieces. Luxury cakes today may not compare with such works of art, but richly decorated syrup-soaked sponges, crumbly pastries, fragile meringues, and crisp choux puffs, filled with cream, chocolate, nuts, and liqueurs, still make unrivaled centerpieces at the dinner table.

Esterházy Cream Torte

Layers of light almond cake are sandwiched together with a creamy and mildly alcoholic filling. Toasted almonds decorate the sides and add a delicate crunch. This cake is mouthwatering, rich, and always impressive.

A crown of fresh, sugar-frosted grapes

Special Ingredients

Lemon peel *flavors the almond sponge.*

Almonds *add a buttery character to the cake.*

Grapes *introduce a fresh flavor and smooth texture.*

Gelatin *stabilizes and firmly sets the frothy wine and cream filling.*

Sweet white wines *like Marsala have full-bodied flavors.*

Dark rum *gives both depth and richness of flavor to the sweet wine in the cream layer.*

Making the Cake

*A*n *Austrian recipe of 1899 named in honor of the princely Magyar family Esterházy. Egg yolks, sugar, and a sweet, quality wine are whipped over heat into a type of zabaglione; cream and rum are added, and the blend of flavors combined with the almond sponge is splendid.*

INGREDIENTS

For the cake

1 quantity Whipped Almond Cake (see page 105)

For the filling

3 tbsp water

1 tbsp unflavored gelatin

1¼ cups (300ml) heavy cream

2 tbsp dark rum

4 egg yolks

½ cup (125g) granulated sugar

½ cup plus 2 tbsp (150ml) sweet white wine, such as Marsala or Sauternes

For the decoration

1¼ cups (450ml) heavy cream, whipped

1 cup (125g) toasted sliced almonds

2–3 tbsp confectioners' sugar

6oz (180g) frosted green grapes (see page 148)

1 Make the almond cake in the prepared 9½in (24cm) pan (see page 105). Bake in the preheated oven for 1 hour and let cool. Cut horizontally into two layers and place the bottom half in the bottom of the prepared 8½in (22cm) pan.

2 For the filling, put the water in a small bowl, sprinkle with the gelatin, and leave for 5 minutes. Set the bowl in a pan of simmering water and let stand until clear (see page 45). Remove and let cool slightly. Whip the cream with the rum into soft peaks. Set aside.

3 Put the egg yolks and sugar in a large heatproof bowl. Whisk until pale and creamy. Add the wine, rest the bowl over a large pan of simmering water, and whisk until the mixture is thick and mousselike. Take the pan off the heat and continue whisking over the water until the mixture has thickened even more. Lift off the bowl and place it in a larger bowl filled with iced water. Whisk until the mixture reaches the ribbon stage (see page 48) and is cool.

4 Slowly whisk the dissolved gelatin into the mousse mixture. Gently fold in the rum-flavored whipped cream. Set aside a quarter of the mixture. Pour the remainder into the pan and cover with the top layer of the cake. Spread the remaining mixture over the top of the cake and chill for 3–4 hours, until set.

5 Remove the cake from the pan and transfer to a plate. For the decoration, spoon a quarter of the whipped cream into a pastry bag fitted with a ½in (1cm) star nozzle. Spread the rest around the side of the cake and press on the almonds (see page 143). Mark a diamond pattern on top with a knife and dust with confectioners' sugar. Pipe small stars of cream (see page 145) around the top of the cake and finish with the grapes.

Oven temperature
325°F/160°C

Baking time
1 hour

Cake pans
One 9½in (24cm) springform pan, greased and lined for the cake; one 8½in (22cm) springform pan, lightly oiled, in which to assemble the torte

Makes
12 slices

Storage
Keeps for 2–3 days

Step ahead
Make the almond cake; prepare the frosted grapes

Mozart Torte

Wolfgang Amadeus Mozart was the inspiration for this lovely dessert. A delicate almond and apricot sponge is soaked with Cointreau-flavored syrup and then layered with an almond Japonais. It is finished with a thick coating of chocolate ganache, then a layer of whipped cream.

INGREDIENTS

For the base

½ quantity Japonais mixture (see page 117) made with ground almonds

For the cake

¾ cup (90g) ground almonds

¾ cup (100g) confectioners' sugar, sifted

4 egg whites

5 egg yolks

pinch of salt

1 tbsp water

2 tsp finely grated lemon zest

½ cup (100g) granulated sugar

2 tbsp cornstarch, sifted

½ cup (60g) all-purpose flour, sifted

5oz (150g) canned apricots, drained and chopped

2 tbsp butter, melted and cooled slightly

For the filling and decoration

1 quantity chocolate ganache (see page 151)

4 tbsp Cointreau-flavored syrup (see page 153)

1¼ cups (300ml) heavy cream

chocolate curls (see page 147)

1 For the base, make the Japonais mixture with ground almonds instead of ground hazelnuts (see page 117). Spread evenly on the bottom of the prepared pan and bake in the preheated oven for 1 hour. Remove from the oven and set the pan on a wire rack to cool. Turn out of the pan and peel off the lining paper. Wash and reline the pan. Raise the oven temperature.

2 For the cake, put the almonds and confectioners' sugar in a large bowl. Stir in 1 egg white to make a smooth, stiff paste. Beat in the egg yolks, one at a time, followed by the salt, water, and lemon zest.

3 In another bowl, whisk the remaining egg whites into stiff peaks. Gradually whisk in half the granulated sugar to form a stiff, glossy meringue (see page 49). Gently fold in the remaining granulated sugar and the sifted cornstarch.

4 Gently fold the flour into the almond mixture, followed by the apricots and melted butter, taking care not to add any of the milky liquid that collects in the bottom of the pan. Fold 2 large spoonfuls of the meringue into the almond mixture to loosen the texture, then carefully fold in the remainder until everything is evenly mixed.

5 Pour the mixture into the prepared pan and lightly level the surface. Bake in the preheated oven for 50 minutes, or until golden and a skewer inserted into the cake comes out clean. Let stand in the pan for 10 minutes. Invert onto a wire rack, carefully peel off the lining paper, and let cool.

TO FINISH THE CAKE

1 Place the Japonais layer on a serving plate and spread with a ¼in (5mm) thick layer of the chocolate ganache. Cover with the almond and apricot sponge. Sprinkle the surface of the sponge evenly with the Cointreau-flavored syrup and let stand for 5–10 minutes to allow the syrup to soak in.

2 Spread the remaining ganache over the top and sides of the cake in an even layer (see page 142). Chill for 1 hour, or until the ganache has set.

3 Whip the cream into stiff peaks. Carefully spread it evenly over the top and sides of the cake using a narrow spatula, making sure that none of the chocolate ganache shows through. Sprinkle the top of the cake generously with chocolate curls to decorate. Chill overnight before serving.

 Oven temperature
325°F/160°C for the Japonais base; 350°F/180°C for the cake

 Baking time
1 hour for the Japonais base; 50 minutes for the cake

 Cake pan
8½in (22cm) springform pan, greased and lined

 Makes
12–16 slices

 Storage
Chill overnight before serving; keeps for 3 days

Step ahead
Make the chocolate ganache and Cointreau-flavored syrup

Rum & Citrus Torte

A rich torte, this is typical of those popular in 19th-century Austria and Germany, which were flavored with alcohol. Here, the whole cake is coated with a lemon-flavored glacé icing and decorated with pistachio nuts and curls of coarse orange and lemon zest. (See page 13 for illustration.)

INGREDIENTS

For the cake

1 quantity Biscuit de Savoie sponge mixture (see page 65)

1 tsp finely grated orange zest

1 tsp finely grated lemon zest

For the filling

3 egg whites

1¼ cups (150g) confectioners' sugar

1 cup (250g) unsalted butter, softened

1 tbsp dark rum

1 tbsp finely grated orange zest

orange and green liquid food coloring (optional)

3 tbsp blanched pistachio nuts (see page 45), finely chopped

9 tbsp (135ml) rum and citrus-flavored syrup (see page 155)

For the decoration

4–5 tbsp (60–75ml) apricot glaze (see page 149)

2 quantities lemon glacé icing (see page 152)

¼ cup (30g) blanched pistachio nuts (see page 45), halved

coarse strands of orange and lemon zest (see page 149)

1 Make the cake mixture (see page 65), adding the orange and lemon zest to the whisked egg yolks and sugar. Pour the mixture equally into the prepared pans and bake in the preheated oven for 20 minutes, or until a skewer inserted into each of the cakes comes out clean. Remove from the oven and let rest in the pans for 5–10 minutes. Invert onto a wire rack and let cool. Peel off the lining paper.

2 For the filling, put the egg whites and sugar in a large heatproof bowl. Rest over a large pan of simmering water and whisk vigorously for 3 minutes, or until a stiff meringue forms. Take the pan off the heat and whisk the mixture for another 1–2 minutes. Transfer the mixture to a cold bowl and let cool.

3 In another bowl, beat the butter until pale and fluffy. Gradually beat in the meringue mixture, one spoonful at a time, until well combined. Slowly beat in the rum.

4 Spoon a third of the mixture into another bowl and beat in the orange zest and a little orange food coloring if using. Stir the pistachio nuts and a little green food coloring, if using, into the larger amount. Cover both bowls with plastic wrap and chill for 15 minutes.

TO FINISH THE CAKE

1 Slice each cake horizontally in half. Sprinkle the cut side of each layer evenly with one quarter of the rum and citrus-flavored syrup. Let stand for 5–10 minutes.

2 Place the bottom layer of one cake on a board and spread with half the pistachio buttercream. Cover with the next cake layer and spread with the orange buttercream. Cover with the bottom layer of the second cake and spread with the remaining pistachio-flavored buttercream. Cover with the remaining cake layer. Press the layers together gently but firmly to bind well and then even up the sides of the cake to give a smooth surface (see page 52).

3 Place the cake on a wire rack set over a plate. Brush the top and sides of the cake with the apricot glaze and let stand for 5 minutes to set.

4 To decorate, pour the glacé icing onto the cake and spread evenly over the top and sides with a narrow spatula (see page 142). Sprinkle the top with the halved pistachio nuts and the strands of orange and lemon zest and let set. Transfer the cake to a plate and let stand overnight before serving.

Oven temperature
350°F/180°C

Baking time
20 minutes

Cake pans
Two 8½in (22cm) springform pans, greased and lined

Makes
8–10 slices

Storage
Let stand overnight before serving; keeps for 4–5 days

Dobos Torta

The Hungarian pastry chef József C. Dobos created this lovely torta in 1906 and donated the recipe to the local Pastry and Honey-Breadmakers Guild. Layers of sponge are sandwiched together with a rich chocolate buttercream, and the whole cake is topped with distinctive honey-brown wedges of caramel. (See page 12 for illustration.)

INGREDIENTS

For the cake

⅔ cup (75g) all-purpose flour
½ cup (75g) potato starch
⅔ cup (150g) granulated sugar
6 eggs, separated
1 tsp finely grated lemon or orange zest

For the filling and decoration

3 quantities quick chocolate buttercream (see page 151)
1 tsp butter
¾ cup (180g) granulated sugar
3 drops of lemon juice

1 For the cake, sift together the all-purpose flour and potato starch and set aside. Set aside two thirds of the granulated sugar. Whisk the egg yolks with the remaining sugar to the ribbon stage (see page 48). Whisk in the citrus zest.

2 In another bowl, whisk the egg whites into soft peaks. Gradually whisk in the reserved sugar to form stiff, glossy peaks (see page 49). Stir 2 large spoonfuls of the egg whites into the egg yolk mixture to loosen the texture. Gently fold in the flour, followed by the remaining egg whites, taking care not to deflate them.

3 Divide one third of the cake mixture between the two prepared pans. Spread in an even layer over the bottom of each one, using the back of a spoon. Bake in the preheated oven for 5–6 minutes, until lightly golden.

4 Remove the cakes from the oven and loosen the edges of each one with a small narrow spatula. Carefully invert onto wire racks, peel off the lining paper, cover with clean sheets of paper, and let cool. Reline the pans and repeat the process twice more with the remaining mixture to make another four thin layers of sponge, making six in total.

TO FINISH THE CAKE

1 Set aside one quarter of the quick chocolate buttercream. Sandwich each of the six sponge layers together with a ¼ in (5mm) thick layer of the buttercream (see page 52), then spread more buttercream evenly over the top and sides of the cake (see page 142). Chill for 1 hour before decorating.

2 For the caramel decoration, draw an 8½ in (22cm) circle on a sheet of waxed paper. Mark it into eight or twelve even-sized wedges. Melt the butter in a heavy-bottomed pan. Add the sugar and the lemon juice and heat gently, stirring occasionally, until a golden caramel has formed.

3 Pour the caramel into the center of the marked circle and quickly spread it out using a hot, clean narrow spatula. Leave for a few seconds until it is just starting to set. Then cut into eight or twelve wedges, using the marked lines as a guide, with a large, lightly greased sharp knife. Remember to regrease the knife with butter between each cut. Let the caramel cool until hard.

4 Spoon the reserved buttercream into a pastry bag fitted with a ½ in (1cm) star nozzle. Pipe eight or twelve large rosettes (see page 145) at even intervals around the top edge of the cake. Rest a caramel wedge at an angle on each one.

 Oven temperature
425°F/220°C

 Baking time
5–6 minutes for each batch

 Cake pans
Two 8½ in (22cm) round pans, greased and lined

 Makes
8–12 slices

 Storage
Keeps for 4–5 days in a cool place; do not refrigerate

 Step ahead
Make the quick chocolate buttercream

Hazelnut Macaroon Cake

This is probably the dessert that inspires the most effusive compliments of all; it is quite irresistible. Four deliciously crunchy hazelnut-meringue layers are luxuriously sandwiched with a plain disk of meringue and filled with a luscious chocolate cream ganache.

INGREDIENTS

For the meringue layers

1 quantity Simple Meringues (see page 112)

6 egg whites

1½ cups (375g) superfine sugar

3 cups (375g) toasted hazelnuts (see page 45), finely ground

4 tsp cocoa powder

For the filling and decoration

3 quantities chocolate ganache (see page 151)

chocolate curls (see page 147)

1 Make the Simple Meringues mixture and spread it into the prepared pan. Bake in the preheated oven for 1½ hours, or until crisp and dry. Remove from the oven, loosen the edges with a narrow spatula, lift out of the pan, and let cool on a wire rack.

2 Whisk 3 of the egg whites into soft peaks. Gradually whisk in half the sugar to form a stiff, glossy meringue (see page 49). Mix half the hazelnuts with 2 teaspoons of the cocoa and gently fold in. Spoon the mixture on the prepared baking sheets and spread out evenly within the marked circles (see page 49).

3 Bake in the preheated oven for 1 hour, or until crisp and dry. Remove from the oven and let cool on wire racks. Reline the baking sheets and repeat the process with the rest of the ingredients to make two more disks. Peel off the lining paper once the meringues are cold.

4 To assemble the cake, set aside half the ganache. Use the rest to sandwich together the meringue disks, with the plain disk in the center. Spoon one third of the reserved ganache into a pastry bag fitted with a ¼in (5mm) plain nozzle. Spread the rest over the top and sides of the cake (see page 142). Mark the sides with a confectionery comb (see page 143).

5 Mark the top of the cake into twelve wedges. Pipe beads of ganache around the base and top of the cake, then along the marked lines. Fill each segment with the chocolate curls. Chill for 2 hours before serving.

Oven temperature
275°F/140°C

Baking time
1½ hours for the plain meringue; 1 hour for the hazelnut-meringue disks

Cake pans
9in (23cm) springform pan, greased and lined; two flat baking sheets, each lined with waxed paper and marked with a 9in (23cm) circle

Makes
12 slices

Storage
Keeps for 3 days in the refrigerator

Freezing
Freezes for 1–2 months, undecorated

Step ahead
Prepare the toasted hazelnuts; make the chocolate ganache

Gâteau Saint Honoré

This cake is named after the patron saint of pastry chefs and bakers. A crown of choux pastry, made with milk and water to give a soft crust, is baked on a shortcrust pastry base and filled with crème pâtissière. A pretty circlet of small caramelized choux pastry puffs is set on the crown. Assemble and finish this cake no more than 2–3 hours before serving.

INGREDIENTS

1 quantity pâte sucrée pastry (see page 55)

For the choux pastry

1 quantity choux pastry made with ½ cup (125ml) each milk and water (see page 57)

1 egg yolk

For the caramel glaze

scant 1 cup (200g) granulated sugar

3 tbsp water

For the filling

⅔ cup (150ml) heavy cream

2 tsp granulated sugar

2 quantities crème pâtissière (see page 151)

1 Allow the pâte sucrée pastry to come back to room temperature. Knead briefly until smooth and then roll out on a lightly floured surface into a 9in (23cm) circle. Place on the greased baking sheet, prick all over with a fork, and chill until ready to use.

2 Make the choux pastry. Spoon into a pastry bag fitted with a ½in (1cm) plain nozzle. Mix the remaining beaten egg left over from making the choux pastry with the egg yolk and use a little to brush a 1in (2.5cm) strip around the edge of the chilled pastry circle. Pipe some of the choux pastry in a raised, thick band around the outside edge of the pastry.

3 Pipe the remaining choux pastry into 14–16 small 1in (2.5cm) mounds on the wet baking sheet (see page 57). Brush both these puffs and the choux pastry ring with the remaining beaten egg mixture.

4 Bake the choux puffs in the preheated oven for about 20 minutes, or until crisp and golden. Remove from the oven and pierce a hole in the bottom of each one with a fine metal skewer. Return the puffs to the oven, upside down, for 5 minutes. Transfer the puffs to a wire rack and let cool.

5 Bake the pastry and choux base in the preheated oven for 10 minutes. Lower the oven temperature and cook for 20 minutes more, or until both the pastry base and the choux circle are golden brown. Remove from the oven, prick the choux pastry in several places to release the steam, and return to the oven for 5 minutes. Transfer to a wire rack and let cool.

TO FINISH THE CAKE

1 Make the caramel glaze (see page 153). As soon as the syrup is amber-colored, plunge the bottom of the pan into cold water to stop it from cooking further. Set aside in a bowl of very hot water to keep the caramel liquid. Carefully dip the top of each choux puff into the caramel (see step 1 opposite), place in a single layer on a wire rack, caramel side up, and let set.

2 For the filling, whip the cream and sugar together into stiff peaks. Spoon into a pastry bag fitted with a ¼in (5mm) plain nozzle. Pipe into each puff through the hole in the bottom (see step 2 opposite).

3 If the caramel has set, place the pan over low heat and heat gently until it is liquid again. Holding the top of each puff, quickly dip the bottom into the caramel and arrange side by side around the top of the choux ring (see step 3 opposite). Transfer the gâteau to a plate.

4 Spoon the crème pâtissière into a pastry bag fitted with a ½in (1cm) star nozzle. Pipe in a rope design (see page 145) into the center of the gâteau. Chill for 1 hour, or until ready to serve.

Oven temperature
425°F/220°C, then 350°F/180°C

Baking time
25 minutes for the choux puffs; 35 minutes for the pastry and choux base

Cake pans
Two large, flat baking sheets, lightly greased; one run under cold water and left slightly wet

Makes
6–8 slices

Storage
Best eaten within 2–3 hours of assembly

Step ahead
Make the pâte sucrée pastry and crème pâtissière a day ahead; make the choux pastry a few hours beforehand

Glazing Choux Puffs

1 Spear each choux puff with the tip of a small sharp knife. Dip the top into the caramel and let set.

2 Pipe the whipped cream into each choux puff through the hole in the bottom, until the puff feels firm and full.

3 Dip the bottom of each puff quickly into the caramel and arrange side by side around the top of the choux ring.

The finished gâteau

The piped crème pâtissière gives a decorative finish

Chocolate Cakes

Nothing inspires descriptive indulgence quite as much as chocolate: "Pure, delicious, refreshing, stimulating, light, and refined," so the words of an early 20th-century advertisment pointed out, defining its great medicinal virtues. The best chocolate cakes excite the taste buds with the suggestion of luscious, warming sweetness, enticing both the palate and the eye. Chocolate combined with different blends of nuts and seeds, fruit, creams, coffee and spices, and spirits and liqueurs becomes wickedly sinful and delicious, and an absolute joy to eat.

Sour Cherry & Chocolate Torte

The layered combination of fresh black cherries, kirsch, chocolate, and cream has long been popular in the dessert repertoire. Here is a more unusual variation using a crunchy hazelnut Japonais layer in the middle of more traditional chocolate layers. For a very simple cake, the basic chocolate sponge can be sandwiched together with whipped cream or chocolate buttercream.

INGREDIENTS

For the cake

1 tsp instant coffee
1½ tbsp boiling water
1½ oz (45g) semisweet chocolate
⅔ cup (90g) all-purpose flour, sifted
1 tbsp cocoa powder
½ tsp ground cinnamon
3 eggs, separated
½ cup (90g) light brown sugar
6 tbsp (90g) unsalted butter, melted and cooled
½ quantity Japonais mixture (see page 117)

For the filling and decoration

3½ cups (900ml) heavy cream
6 tbsp granulated sugar
4 tbsp dark rum or kirsch
6 tbsp (90ml) kirsch-flavored syrup (see page 155)
1½ lb (750g) fresh black cherries, pitted
2½ oz (75g) semisweet chocolate, coarsely grated (see page 147)
1 quantity chocolate caraque (see page 146)
12 fresh cherries with leaves

1 For the cake, dissolve the coffee in the water then melt with the chocolate (see page 44). Let cool. Sift together the flour, cocoa, and cinnamon.

2 Whisk the egg yolks and sugar until fluffy. Stir in the chocolate. Whisk the egg whites into soft peaks. Stir 2 spoonfuls into the egg yolk mixture to loosen the texture. Fold in the flour, butter, and remaining egg whites until evenly mixed.

3 Spoon the mixture into the prepared pan and bake in the preheated oven for 25 minutes. Remove from the oven and let stand for 5 minutes. Invert onto a wire rack, peel off the lining paper, and let cool. Reline the pan and lower the oven temperature.

4 Make the Japonais (see page 117). Spread into the pan and bake for 1 hour. Remove from oven and let cool.

TO FINISH THE CAKE

1 Whip the cream, sugar, and rum or kirsch into soft peaks. Set aside two thirds. Slice the cake horizontally in half and sprinkle each layer with syrup. Place half the cherries on the bottom layer, then spread with half the remaining cream. Cover with the Japonais. Scatter over the remaining cherries, spread with the rest of the cream, and cover with the top cake layer.

2 Spread two thirds of reserved cream over the cake. Coat the sides with the grated chocolate (see page 143). Spoon the rest of the cream into a pastry bag fitted with a ½in (1cm) star nozzle and pipe shells around the top (see page 145). Finish with caraque and cherries. Chill for 3–4 hours.

Oven temperature
350°F/180°C for the cake; 325°F/160°C for the Japonais

Baking time
25 minutes for the cake; 1 hour for the Japonais

Cake pan
8½in (22cm) round pan, greased and lined

Makes
12–16 slices

Storage
Keeps for 3–4 days in the refrigerator

Freezing
Freezes for 1–2 months, undecorated

Special Ingredients

Semisweet chocolate should contain at least 70% cocoa solids for the richest flavor.

Hazelnuts, lightly toasted, add texture and flavor to the Japonais layer.

Fresh cherries taste best. Use canned cherries if fresh are unavailable.

Cocoa powder costs less than chocolate and gives depth of flavor to the sponge.

Cinnamon has a sweet, woody, and intense aroma that enhances the chocolate.

Dark rum adds a mellow note and gives a punch to the chocolate layers.

Fresh cream piped in a shell design

Fresh cherries, cherry leaves, and chocolate caraque make a stunning decoration

Chocolate Fortissimo

This is a moist, rich cake that might have been especially developed for chocoholics. Assemble it at least a day before it is needed so that the flavors have time to blend.

INGREDIENTS

For the cake

2 quantities chocolate cake mixture (see Sour Cherry & Chocolate Torte page 78)

For the truffles

2 tsp instant coffee

2 tbsp Tia Maria

4oz (125g) semisweet chocolate

4 tbsp unsalted butter

2 tbsp confectioners' sugar, sifted

1 tbsp heavy cream

3–4 tbsp cocoa powder

For the filling and decoration

⅔ cup (150ml) heavy cream

2 tsp granulated sugar

1 tbsp Tia Maria or dark rum

6 tbsp (90ml) Tia Maria-flavored syrup (see page 155)

2 quantities quick chocolate buttercream (see page 151)

1 Make the chocolate cake mixture (see page 78). Divide between the prepared pans and bake in the preheated oven for 25 minutes, or until a skewer inserted into each cake comes out clean. Remove from the oven and let cool on a wire rack. Turn out of the pans and peel off the lining paper.

2 For the truffles, dissolve the coffee in the Tia Maria. Melt the chocolate with the dissolved coffee (see page 44). Let cool. Beat the butter and sugar together. Beat in the chocolate mixture and the cream. Chill for 40 minutes. Shape the mixture into 14 even-sized balls, dust in the cocoa powder, and chill for 2 hours (see steps 1–3 below).

3 For the filling, whip the cream, sugar, and Tia Maria into stiff peaks. Cover and chill.

TO FINISH THE CAKE

1 Slice each cake horizontally in half and sprinkle each cut side with one quarter of the Tia Maria-flavored syrup.

2 Spoon one quarter of the chocolate buttercream into a pastry bag fitted with a ½in (1cm) star nozzle. Reserve half the remainder. Set both aside.

3 Sandwich together the cake layers in pairs using the rest of the buttercream (see page 52). Sandwich these together with the whipped cream.

4 For the decoration, spread the reserved buttercream over the cake (see page 142). Pipe 14 rosettes of buttercream around the top edge (see page 145) and rest a truffle on each. Chill overnight before serving.

 Oven temperature 350°F/180°C

 Baking time 25 minutes

 Cake pans Two 8½in (22cm) round pans, greased and lined

 Makes 14 slices

 Storage Leave for 1 day before serving; keeps for 1 week

 Freezing Freezes for 1–2 months, undecorated

Step ahead Make the truffles and chill for 2 hours; make the Tia Maria-flavored syrup and the quick chocolate buttercream

Making Chocolate Truffles

1 *Divide the mixture into 14 pieces. Dust your fingers with cocoa powder, then lightly roll each piece to make a ball. If the balls are soft, chill them until firm.*

2 *To coat the truffles, sift the cocoa powder into a medium-sized bowl. Drop in three truffles at a time and gently swirl the bowl until each one is evenly coated.*

3 *Carefully lift the truffles out of the bowl and lay them, spaced a little apart, on a baking sheet lined with waxed paper. Chill for 2 hours, or until firm.*

Orange & Chocolate Layer Cake

Containing just a hint of chocolate blended with almond, this fine-textured cake has an attractive color. The tang of the orange in the buttercream filling provides a delicious contrast.

INGREDIENTS

For the cake

½ cup (90g) granulated sugar

6 eggs, separated

⅓ cup (60g) light brown sugar

½ cup (60g) all-purpose flour

4 tbsp cocoa powder

1 cup (100g) ground almonds

1 tbsp unsalted butter, melted

For the filling and decoration

2½ quantities orange mousseline buttercream (see page 150)

10–12 chocolate fans (see page 145)

1 For the cake, set aside 2 tablespoons of the granulated sugar. Whisk the egg yolks, remaining granulated sugar, and light brown sugar together until thick and mousselike.

2 Sift the flour and cocoa powder together twice. Gently fold into the egg yolk mixture, followed by the ground almonds and the melted butter, taking care not to add any of the milky liquid that collects in the bottom of the pan.

3 In another bowl, whisk the egg whites into soft peaks (see page 47). Whisk in the reserved sugar. Stir 2 large spoonfuls into the main mixture to loosen the texture, then gently fold in the remainder, taking care not to deflate the whites.

4 Pour the mixture into the prepared pans and bake in the preheated oven for about 25 minutes, or until a skewer inserted into each cake comes out clean. Remove from the oven and let rest in the pans for 5 minutes. Invert onto a wire rack, peel off the lining paper, and let cool.

TO FINISH THE CAKE

1 Slice each cake horizontally in half. Spoon one fifth of the buttercream into a pastry bag fitted with a ½in (1cm) star nozzle. Sandwich the cake layers together with half the remaining buttercream.

2 Spread the rest of the buttercream over the top and sides of the cake. Mark the sides into lines with a confectionery comb (see page 143). Carefully pipe the reserved buttercream in a rope design around the top of the cake (see page 145) and add the chocolate fans.

 Oven temperature
350°F/180°C

 Baking time
25 minutes

 Cake pans
Two 8½in (22cm) springform pans, greased and lined

 Makes
16 slices

 Storage
Keeps for 3–4 days

 Freezing
Freezes for 1–2 months, undecorated

 Step ahead
Make the orange mousseline buttercream and the chocolate fans

Fudge Squares

These squares are very easy to make. All the ingredients are simply mixed together in one large bowl with an electric mixer. The finished texture of the cake is very rich and fudgy.

INGREDIENTS

8oz (250g) semisweet chocolate

½ cup (125g) butter, softened and cut into small pieces

4 eggs, lightly beaten

⅔ cup (150g) granulated sugar

½ cup (75g) self-rising flour, sifted

confectioners' sugar to decorate

1 Melt the chocolate in a heat-proof bowl (see page 44) and let cool. Put the butter, eggs, granulated sugar, and flour in a large bowl. Add the cooled chocolate and beat slowly until everything is evenly mixed.

2 Continue to beat the mixture more quickly for about 10 minutes, until it has thickened, increased in volume, and become much paler in color.

3 Pour the mixture into the prepared pan and bake in the preheated oven for ¾–1 hour. The cake will be fudgy at ¾ hour, more cakelike at 1 hour.

4 Remove from the oven and cool on a wire rack. Take out of the pan, peel off the lining paper, and cut into squares. Dust with confectioners' sugar.

 Oven temperature
350°F/180°C

 Baking time
¾–1 hour

 Cake pan
8½in (22cm) square pan, greased and lined

 Makes
16–24 squares

 Storage
Keep for 4–5 days

Freezing
Freeze for 1–2 months

Chocolate Chestnut Roulade

A soft jelly roll with a difference. Almonds lend bite to this mixture, and butter moistness, so the cake can be rolled up when cold.

INGREDIENTS

For the cake

3oz (90g) semisweet chocolate

4 eggs, separated

2 tbsp granulated sugar

1 tbsp confectioners' sugar

¼ cup (45g) unblanched almonds, very finely chopped

3 tbsp butter, melted and cooled

For the filling and decoration

2 tsp cocoa powder

1 tsp confectioners' sugar

1 quantity chestnut buttercream (see page 150)

⅔ cup (150ml) heavy cream, whipped

chocolate curls (see page 147)

3 marrons glacés, halved

1 For the cake, melt the chocolate (see page 44) and let cool. Whisk the egg yolks and granulated sugar together to the ribbon stage (see page 48).

2 In another bowl, whisk the egg whites into soft peaks (see page 47). Sift over the confectioners' sugar and whisk to form slightly stiffer peaks. Stir the chocolate, nuts, and butter into the main mixture. Gently fold in the egg whites, taking care not to deflate them.

3 Pour the mixture into the prepared pan and level the surface. Bake in the preheated oven for 15–20 minutes, until soft and springy to the touch. Remove from the oven and cover with waxed paper and a damp dish towel. Let cool.

4 Sift the cocoa powder and confectioners' sugar onto more waxed paper. Uncover the roulade and invert onto it. Peel off the lining paper and spread over the buttercream to within ½in (1cm) of the edge (see page 53). Roll up from a short edge, and place seam down on a plate.

5 Spoon the cream into a pastry bag fitted with a ½in (1cm) star nozzle. Pipe a scroll down the center of the cake (see page 145). Finish with chocolate curls and marrons glacés.

 Oven temperature
350°F/180°C

 Baking time
15–20 minutes

 Cake pan
15x10x¾in (38x25x2cm) jelly roll pan, greased and lined

Makes
12 slices

Storage
Keeps for 3–4 days

Freezing
Freezes for 1 month, undecorated

Step ahead
Make the chestnut buttercream

Warning
This recipe contains raw eggs (see page 9)

Moist Chocolate & Hazelnut Cake

My sister Annette loves to bake, and this recipe, my brother-in-law's absolute favorite, is from her repertoire. The cake is made without flour.

INGREDIENTS

For the cake

6oz (180g) semisweet chocolate

¾ cup (180g) granulated sugar

¾ cup (180g) butter

6 eggs, separated

2½ cups (180g) toasted hazelnuts, ground

For the decoration

2 tbsp apricot glaze (see page 149)

3½ oz (100g) semisweet chocolate

1 tbsp butter

2 tbsp water

chopped toasted hazelnuts

1 Melt the chocolate (see page 44) and let cool. Beat all but 3 tablespoons sugar with the butter until pale and fluffy. Mix in the egg yolks and chocolate.

2 In another bowl, whisk the egg whites into soft peaks. Whisk in the reserved sugar. Stir 2 spoonfuls into the main mixture. Gently fold in the nuts and remaining egg whites.

3 Pour the mixture into the prepared pan and bake in the preheated oven for 45–55 minutes, or until a skewer comes out clean. Remove from the oven and let stand for 5 minutes. Invert onto a wire rack and peel off the lining paper. Brush the top with the glaze and let cool.

4 Melt the chocolate with the butter and water. Pour onto the cake and spread over the top and sides. Sprinkle with the chopped nuts and let set.

 Oven temperature
350°F/180°C

 Baking time
45–55 minutes

 Cake pan
9in (23cm) springform pan, greased and lined

 Makes
12 slices

 Storage
Keeps for 1 week

 Freezing
Freezes for 1–2 months, undecorated

 Step ahead
Prepare the toasted hazelnuts (see page 45)

Nutty Brownies

Brownies must always be dense, dark, soft, and fudgy, studded with nuts, and full of rich chocolate.

INGREDIENTS

2oz (60g) semisweet chocolate

½ cup (125g) butter

½ cup (60g) all-purpose flour

pinch of salt

2 eggs

¾ cup (180g) dark brown sugar

½ tsp vanilla extract

¾ cup (125g) walnuts or pecans, coarsely chopped)

1 Melt the chocolate with the butter (see page 44) and let cool. Sift together the flour and salt and set aside.

2 In another bowl, whisk the eggs and sugar together to the ribbon stage (see page 48). Stir in the melted chocolate and the vanilla extract.

3 Gently fold alternating spoonfuls of the flour and the chopped nuts into the chocolate mixture until everything is evenly mixed.

4 Pour the mixture into the prepared pan and bake in the preheated oven for 25 minutes, until the top is shiny and firm but the center is still slightly soft. Remove from the oven and let cool in the pan on a wire rack. Turn out of the pan, peel off the lining paper, and cut into even-sized squares to serve.

 Oven temperature
350°F/180°C

 Baking time
25 minutes

 Cake pan
8in (20cm) shallow square pan, greased and lined

 Makes
9–12 squares

Storage
Keep for 1 week

Freezing
Freeze for 1–2 months

Sacher Torte

A variation on the classic Viennese confection created by Franz Sacher in 1832 for Prince Metternich. The original recipe has been kept a closely guarded secret and is still the subject of litigation – but it is probably the most famous chocolate cake in the world. (See page 15 for illustration.)

INGREDIENTS

For the cake

4oz (125g) semisweet chocolate

¾ cup (100g) sifted confectioners' sugar

7 tbsp (100g) unsalted butter

5 egg yolks

½ tsp vanilla extract

4 egg whites

¾ cup (100g) ground almonds

3 tbsp sifted cake flour

For the decoration

2 tbsp apricot glaze (see page 149)

1 quantity rich chocolate icing (see page 147)

chocolate leaves (see page 146)

1 For the cake, melt the chocolate (see page 44) and let cool slightly. Reserve 2 tablespoons of the sugar. Beat the remainder with the butter until pale and fluffy. Beat in the egg yolks, one at a time. Stir in the vanilla and chocolate.

2 In another bowl, whisk the egg whites into soft peaks. Whisk in the reserved sugar. Stir 2 large spoonfuls into the main mixture to loosen the texture.

3 Fold in alternating spoonfuls of almonds and flour. Gently fold in the remaining egg whites, until everything is evenly mixed.

4 Pour the mixture into the prepared pan and lightly level the surface. Rap the pan once on the work surface to disperse any pockets of air that might be trapped in the mixture.

5 Bake in the preheated oven for 45–50 minutes, or until a skewer inserted into the cake comes out clean. Remove from the oven and let rest in the pan for 10 minutes. Invert onto a wire rack, peel off the lining paper, and let cool.

6 For the decoration, place the cake on a wire rack set over a plate and brush the top and sides with the apricot glaze. Pour on the rich chocolate icing and tilt the cake so that the icing coats the top and sides evenly (see page 147). Transfer to a plate and arrange the chocolate leaves around the edge of the cake to decorate. Let set before serving.

 Oven temperature
350°F/180°C

 Baking time
45–50 minutes

 Cake pan
8½in (22cm) springform pan, greased and lined

 Makes
12–16 slices

Storage
Keeps for 4–5 days

Freezing
Freezes for 1–2 months, undecorated

Chocolate Fudge Cake

If you have a penchant for really rich chocolate, this is the cake for you. It only rises a little in baking and tends to drop when cold, but then it develops the most deliciously fudgy texture. It is very good covered with whipped cream, or chocolate rich icing (see page 147), which makes it into a sumptuous dessert.

INGREDIENTS

For the cake

5½ oz (160g) semisweet chocolate

2 tbsp unsalted butter

1 egg yolk

¼ cup (60g) granulated sugar

4 egg whites

For the decoration

⅔ cup (150ml) heavy cream

2oz (60g) semisweet chocolate, finely grated

1 For the cake, melt the chocolate and butter together (see page 44) and let cool.

2 Whisk the egg yolk and 1 tablespoon of the sugar together until pale and fluffy. Stir in the melted chocolate.

3 In another bowl, whisk the egg whites into soft peaks.

Gradually whisk in the rest of the sugar to form stiff, glossy peaks (see page 49). Carefully stir 2 large spoonfuls into the main mixture to loosen the texture, then gently fold in the rest until all is evenly mixed.

4 Pour the mixture into the prepared pan and bake in the preheated oven for about 30–35 minutes, or until a skewer inserted into the cake comes out clean. Remove from the oven and let rest in the pan for 10 minutes. Take out of the pan and let cool on a wire rack.

5 Carefully peel off the lining paper and transfer the cake to a serving plate. Whip the cream into stiff peaks. Spread evenly over the top of the cake and sprinkle with the grated chocolate to decorate.

 Oven temperature
350°F/180°C

 Baking time
30–35 minutes

 Cake pan
8in (20cm) springform pan, greased and lined

 Makes
8 slices

 Storage
Keeps for 3–4 days

 Freezing
Freezes for 1–2 months, undecorated

Caracas

This stylish, elegantly shaped chocolate log is baked in a Balmoral or semi-circular pan (see page 41) and covered with a thick layer of chocolate ganache. It is excellent served with a cup of dark coffee. (See page 14 for illustration.)

INGREDIENTS

For the cake

1oz (30g) semisweet chocolate

1 tbsp cold water

3 eggs, separated

¼ cup (30g) confectioners' sugar, sifted

⅓ cup (45g) ground almonds

1 tbsp granulated sugar

1½ tbsp all-purpose flour, sifted

1½ tbsp butter, melted and cooled

For the filling and decoration

¾ cup (175ml) heavy cream

7oz (200g) semisweet chocolate, grated

10 square chocolate thins, halved

1 For the cake, melt the chocolate with the water (see page 44) and let cool. Whisk the egg yolks and confectioners' sugar to the ribbon stage (see page 48). Stir in the melted chocolate and ground almonds.

2 In another bowl, whisk the egg whites into soft peaks.

Whisk in the granulated sugar. Stir 2 large spoonfuls into the main mixture to loosen the texture. Gently fold in the flour and melted butter, followed by the remaining egg whites.

3 Pour the mixture into the prepared pan and bake in the preheated oven for 25 minutes, or until a skewer inserted into the cake comes out clean. Remove from the oven, invert onto a wire rack, and let cool.

4 Cut a right-angled wedge lengthwise out of the top of the cake. Make the filling as for chocolate ganache (see page 151). Spoon one quarter into a pastry bag fitted with a ½in (1cm) star nozzle. Spread a little ganache into the cavity and replace the wedge. Spread the rest over the cake and mark with horizontal lines. Pipe ganache down the center in 10 swirls and decorate with the chocolate thins.

 Oven temperature
350°F/180°C

 Baking time
25 minutes

 Cake pan
10½ x 4½ in (27x11cm) Balmoral pan or semi-circular pan, greased and floured

 Makes
10 slices

 Storage
Keeps for 1 week

 Freezing
Freezes for 1 month

Poppy Seed & Chocolate Torte

Intensely moist in texture, this Hungarian cake from the 19th century includes poppy seeds, which give an unusual flavor, handsomely complemented by raisins and dark chocolate. Serve with whipped cream on the side.

INGREDIENTS

For the cake

½ cup (90g) raisins

2 tbsp boiling water

3oz (90g) semisweet chocolate

½ cup (125g) butter

½ cup (125g) granulated sugar

1 tsp finely grated lemon zest

6 eggs, separated

2 tbsp toasted bread crumbs, finely ground (see page 45)

1 cup (150g) poppy seeds, finely ground (see Poppy Seed Strudel page 104)

For the filling and decoration

5 tbsp (75ml) black cherry jam, sieved and warmed

1 quantity of rich chocolate icing (see page 147)

4–6 quantities chocolate caraque (see page 146)

confectioners' sugar

1 Soak the raisins in the water for 30 minutes. Drain and pat dry. Melt the chocolate (see page 44) and let cool.

2 Beat the butter, sugar, and lemon zest together until pale and fluffy. Beat in the egg yolks, one at a time, then the chocolate, bread crumbs, and raisins.

3 In another bowl, whisk the egg whites into soft peaks. Stir 2 large spoonfuls into the main mixture to loosen the texture. Gently fold in the poppy seeds and the remaining egg whites until evenly mixed.

4 Pour the mixture carefully into the prepared pan and bake in the preheated oven for 45 minutes, or until a skewer inserted into the cake comes out clean. Invert onto a wire rack, peel off the lining paper, and let cool.

5 Slice the cake horizontally in half and sandwich together with 2 tablespoons of the jam. Spread the remaining jam over the top and sides of the cake. Pour on the rich chocolate icing and tilt to cover (see page 147). Cover the top with the chocolate caraque and let set. Dust with confectioners' sugar just before serving.

 Oven temperature
325°F/160°C

 Baking time
45 minutes

 Cake pan
8½in (22cm) springform pan, greased and lined

 Makes
16–20 slices

 Storage
Keeps for 4–5 days

 Freezing
Freezes for 1–2 months, undecorated

 Step ahead
Soak the raisins; prepare the toasted bread crumbs and the poppy seeds; make the chocolate caraque

Fresh Fruit Cakes

There is something magical about ripe fruit, hanging heavy on the tree bough in a trellis of green foliage. It has inspired us to write and to paint, and of course to cook and to bake. The lavish and abundant harvests in the fruit-growing areas of the world have encouraged cooks to develop many regional specialties, and the resulting combinations of fresh, luscious, brightly colored fruit in cakes and batters have a delicious, mouthwatering appeal that never fails to please the eye and delight the palate.

FRESH PLUM GENOISE, a moist but light and buttery sponge baked between two layers of sliced juicy plums.

Fresh Plum Genoise

The natural juiciness and tartness of plums make this cake moist, but not too sweet. My favorite plums for cooking are the dark red Switzen, which appear only in mid-fall. They are richly flavored and hold their shape well without becoming too watery during baking. Small, blue-purple Italian prune plums and greengages are very successful too.

INGREDIENTS

1¼ lb (625g) plums

For the cake

4 tbsp butter, melted and cooled

½ cup (125g) granulated sugar

4 large eggs, separated

1 tsp finely grated lemon zest

1 cup (125g) all-purpose flour, sifted

granulated sugar to decorate

1 Wash and dry the plums. Cut in half, remove the pits, and slice the flesh thickly. Arrange half the slices over the base of the prepared pan.

2 Make the cake mixture following the method for Rich Genoise Sponge (see page 67). Pour over the plums and bake in the preheated oven for 15 minutes, or until just set.

3 Open the oven door, pull out the shelf with the pan on it, and arrange the remaining plum slices neatly over the top in concentric circles. Slide the shelf back in and cook for 30–45 minutes longer, or until a skewer inserted into the cake comes out clean.

4 Remove from the oven and let cool in the pan. Take the cake out of the pan, peel off the lining paper, and transfer to a serving plate. Dust with a little granulated sugar to decorate. Serve slightly warm or cold with whipped cream.

VARIATION

This sponge can also be made using peeled and cored dessert apples, cut into ¼in (5mm) thick slices.

 Oven temperature 350°F/180°C

 Baking time 45 minutes–1 hour

 Cake pan 8in (20cm) springform pan, greased, lined, greased once more, and then dusted with flour and sugar

 Makes 8 slices

 Storage Keeps for 2–3 days in the refrigerator

 Freezing Freezes for 1–2 months

Italian Pear & Nut Sponge

INGREDIENTS

1½ lb (750g) firm, ripe pears

2 tbsp lemon juice

1½ cups (225g) all-purpose flour

pinch of salt

1½ tsp baking soda

1 tsp ground ginger

½ cup (125ml) sunflower oil

⅔ cup (165g) granulated sugar

1 egg

1 egg yolk

1 tsp finely grated lemon zest

½ cup (60g) walnuts, coarsely chopped

½ cup (100g) golden raisins

confectioners' sugar to decorate

1 Peel and core the pears and cut into small chunks. Sprinkle with the lemon juice to prevent discoloration. Sift the flour, salt, baking soda, and ginger together. Set aside with the pears.

2 Put the oil, granulated sugar, whole egg, and egg yolk into a bowl and beat together well. Gradually stir in the flour, a spoonful at a time, taking care not to overbeat the mixture.

3 Stir the lemon zest, chopped walnuts, and golden raisins into the mixture, followed by the pear pieces, making sure that everything is evenly mixed.

4 Pour the mixture into the prepared pan and bake in the preheated oven for about 1 hour 10 minutes, or until golden and a skewer inserted into the cake comes out clean. (It may need a little more cooking, depending on the ripeness of the pears.)

5 Remove the cake from the oven and let rest in the pan for 10 minutes. Take the cake out of the pan, carefully peel off the lining paper, and let cool on a wire rack. Transfer to a plate and dust with confectioners' sugar. Serve with whipped cream.

 Oven temperature 350°F/180°C

Baking time 1 hour 10 minutes

Cake pan 8½in (22cm) springform pan, greased and lined

Makes 8 slices

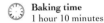 **Storage** Keeps for 2–3 days

 **Freezing** Freezes for 1–2 months

Swiss Black Cherry Cake

A popular cake in the orchard regions of Europe. This is a peasant recipe similar to a French clafouti, a sweet, thick, fruit-laden pancake. The recipe includes ground almonds and bread crumbs to give a richer flavor and enhance its keeping quality.

INGREDIENTS

4 slices (90g) stale white bread

½ cup (100ml) milk, warmed

6 tbsp (90ml) hot water

2 tbsp fresh white bread crumbs

½ cup (125g) granulated sugar

3 eggs, separated

4 tbsp butter, melted and cooled

½ cup (75g) ground almonds

1 tsp ground cinnamon

1½ lb (750g) black or morello cherries, washed, dried, and pitted

pinch of salt

confectioners' sugar to decorate

1 Break the stale bread into small pieces. Put in a bowl, stir in the milk and water, and set aside to soak for 15 minutes. Sprinkle the prepared cake pan with the fresh bread crumbs.

2 Set aside 2 tablespoons of the sugar. Whisk the rest with the egg yolks until smooth. Gradually whisk in the melted butter until the mixture is pale and creamy. Carefully stir in the ground almonds and cinnamon.

3 Drain the bread in a sieve and squeeze out any excess liquid by hand. Beat to a paste with a fork. Stir into the main mixture with the cherries.

4 In another bowl, whisk the egg whites and salt into soft peaks. Sift over the reserved sugar and whisk into slightly stiffer peaks (see page 49). Stir 2 large spoonfuls into the main mixture to loosen the texture, then gently fold in the remainder until evenly mixed.

5 Pour the mixture into the prepared pan and bake in the preheated oven for 1–1¼ hours until golden. Remove from the oven and let rest for 10 minutes. Invert onto a wire rack, peel off the lining paper, and let cool. Dust with a little confectioners' sugar to serve.

 Oven temperature
350°F/180°C

 Baking time
1–1¼ hours

 Cake pan
8½in (22cm) springform pan, greased and lined

 Makes
8–10 slices

 Storage
Keeps for 1–2 days

 Freezing
Freezes for 1–2 months

 Step ahead
Pit the cherries

Devonshire Apple Cake

This simple cake has a moist, puddinglike texture that appeals particularly to children. It comes from a booklet entitled Recipes, Remedies and Rhymes *(1976), which was produced by a group of villagers in Devon, England, to raise funds for their local church. Serve with whipped cream.*

INGREDIENTS

2 quantities apple purée (see page 149)

½ cup (125g) butter, softened

2 eggs, separated

2 cups (125g) fresh white bread crumbs

2 tsp ground cinnamon

5 tbsp (60g) currants

3 tbsp cornstarch, sifted

1 large McIntosh or similar apple

½–1 tbsp granulated sugar

1 Make the apple purée and set aside to cool. Beat the butter and egg yolks together until thick and creamy. Stir in the apple purée, bread crumbs, half the cinnamon, and currants. Sift over the cornstarch and fold in.

2 In another bowl, whisk the egg whites into soft peaks.

Stir 2 large spoonfuls into the main mixture to loosen the texture, then gently fold in the remainder until everything is evenly mixed.

3 Pour the mixture carefully into the prepared pan. Peel, core, and thinly slice the dessert apple. Arrange around the top edge of the cake.

4 Bake in the preheated oven for 1 hour 10 minutes, or until a skewer inserted into the cake comes out clean.

5 Remove from the oven and let cool on a wire rack. Take out of the pan and peel off the lining paper. Transfer to a serving plate and sprinkle with the granulated sugar and the remaining cinnamon to decorate.

 Oven temperature
350°F/180°C

 Baking time
1 hour 10 minutes

 Cake pan
8½in (22cm) springform pan greased, lined, and dusted with sugar and flour

 Makes
8 slices

 Storage
Keeps for 2–3 days

 Freezing
Freezes for 1–2 months

Step ahead
Make the apple purée

Carrot & Hazelnut Loaf

A few years ago I suggested this cake as an entry for our annual village flower and produce show. The first year I baked one myself and persuaded a friend to do the same. Ours were the only entries! The following year there were a few more attempts and it is now a regular feature. Bake it 2–3 days ahead of time to allow the flavors to mature before decorating. (See page 23 for illustration.)

INGREDIENTS

For the cake

1¼ cups (180g) all-purpose flour

1½ tsp baking powder

½ tsp baking soda

pinch of salt

1 tsp ground cinnamon

3 thin (180g) carrots, peeled and grated

¾ cup (90g) toasted hazelnuts, chopped

⅔ cup (150g) light brown sugar

2 eggs

finely grated zest of 1 orange

5 tbsp (75g) butter, melted and cooled

For the decoration

1 quantity cream cheese frosting (see page 150)

16 marzipan carrots (see page 148)

1 tbsp toasted hazelnuts, chopped

coarse strands of orange zest (see page 149)

1 For the cake, sift the flour, baking powder, baking soda, salt, and cinnamon together. Put the carrot in a bowl with the hazelnuts and sugar. Beat in the eggs, one at a time, followed by the orange zest and butter. Gently fold in the flour.

2 Pour the mixture into the prepared pan and bake in the preheated oven for 45 minutes–1 hour, or until a skewer inserted into the cake comes out clean. Remove from the oven and let rest for 10 minutes. Invert onto a wire rack, peel off the lining paper, and let cool completely.

3 Spread the frosting over the top of the cake using a metal spatula. Decorate with the marzipan carrots, nuts, and zest.

Oven temperature
350°F/180°C

Baking time
45 minutes–1 hour

Cake pan
9x5x3in (23x12x7cm) loaf pan, greased and lined

Makes
12 slices

Storage
Keeps for 4–6 days

Pecan & Banana Layer Cake

Many youngsters – and their parents – have a weak spot for all things banana. This rich banana and lime cream filling, taken from Mrs Dull's Georgia cookery book, Southern Cooking (1928), turns the simple banana loaf into a more exciting cake.

INGREDIENTS

For the cake

½ cup (125g) butter

1 cup (250g) light brown sugar

2 large ripe bananas, peeled and mashed

2 eggs, lightly beaten

1 tsp finely grated lime zest

1 tbsp baking soda

2 tbsp boiling water

1 cup (125g) pecans, coarsely chopped

1¼ cups (250g) cake flour, sifted

For the filling

4 medium bananas, peeled and mashed

3 tbsp lime juice

4 tbsp granulated sugar

3 tbsp cornstarch, sifted

For the decoration

⅓ cup (90ml) heavy cream, whipped

1 cup (125g) pecans, finely chopped

1 For the cake, beat the butter and sugar together until pale and fluffy. Gradually beat in the bananas, eggs, and lime zest. Dissolve the baking soda in the boiling water and gently stir in. Carefully mix in the pecans and the flour.

2 Pour the mixture into the prepared pan and bake in the preheated oven for 1 hour, or until a skewer inserted into the cake comes out clean. Remove from the oven and let rest for 10 minutes. Invert onto a wire rack, peel off the lining paper, and let cool.

3 For the filling, push the bananas through a sieve into a heatproof bowl. Stir in the lime juice, granulated sugar, and cornstarch. Rest the bowl over a pan of simmering water and stir for 10 minutes, or until thick. Let cool.

4 Slice the cake horizontally into three layers. Sandwich together with the filling. Spread the whipped cream over the top of the cake and sprinkle with the pecans to decorate.

Oven temperature
350°F/180°C

Baking time
1 hour

Cake pan
9x5x3in (23x12x7cm) loaf pan, greased and lined

Makes
8–10 slices

Storage
Leave to mature for 1 day before serving; keeps for 3–4 days

Freezing
Freezes for 1–2 months, undecorated

Flans & Tarts

A 13th-century Arab manuscript describes a tart filled with a syrupy nut, date, and poppy seed mixture, flavored with rose water, tinted with saffron, and cooked with a roasting chicken suspended above, dripping juices onto the tart. Today flans and tarts excite in a more familiar way. Crisp pastry encases jewel-like berries or citrus slices. Caramelized fruit juices and vanilla creams enhance the flavor and nuts give texture.

French Flan with Red Berries

Rings of colorful, fresh summer berries over a rich and creamy filling within a sweet pastry case look attractive and tempting.

— Making the Flan —

Flavor the crème pâtissière with fresh vanilla if you can. It has a much more subtle and delicate flavor than vanilla extract and the bean can be rinsed off, allowed to dry, and saved for another occasion.

INGREDIENTS

For the flan case

1 quantity pâte sablée pastry (see page 55)

For the filling

2 tbsp apricot jam, sieved

1 quantity crème pâtissière (see page 151)

1½ pints (750ml) strawberries, raspberries, and blueberries or other soft fruit

For the decoration

1 quantity red currant glaze (see page 149)

confectioners' sugar

1 Allow the pastry to come back to room temperature. Knead briefly until smooth, roll out on a lightly floured surface, and use to line the prepared pan (see page 56). Chill for 1 hour.

2 Prick the bottom all over with a fork and bake with pie weights (see page 56) in the preheated oven for 10 minutes. Remove the pie weights and bake for 10–15 minutes longer, or until it is crisp and golden. Remove from the oven and let cool on a wire rack.

3 Brush the pastry case with the apricot jam. Spoon in the crème pâtissière and spread evenly over the base with a small narrow spatula or the back of a spoon. Arrange the prepared fruit close together in concentric circles over the top of the crème pâtissière.

4 Spoon the red currant glaze evenly over the fruit up to the edge of the pastry so that it forms a seal, and let set. Take out of the pan, transfer to a serving plate, and dust the edges of the pastry lightly with confectioners' sugar just before serving.

 Oven temperature
400°F/200°C

 Baking time
20–25 minutes

 Tart pan
9in (23cm) fluted tart pan, greased

 Makes
8 slices

 Storage
Keeps for 1–2 days

 Step ahead
Make the crème pâtissière; make the pastry and chill for 1 hour; make the red currant glaze

Special Ingredients

Mixed berries such as blueberries, raspberries, and strawberries are deliciously sweet yet tart in flavor. They taste best when picked fully ripe. Wash them briefly with their stems intact to retain errant juices, then dry on paper towels. They should not be sugared.

Blueberries

Raspberries

Vanilla beans give the crème pâtissière its wonderful flavor.

Strawberries

Glazed Fresh Orange Flan

This is an unusual and colorful flan filled with freshly glazed oranges. Be sure to score the skin of the oranges thoroughly before simmering the slices in the syrup; otherwise, they become tough and chewy. (See page 19 for illustration.)

INGREDIENTS

For the flan case

1 quantity pâte sablée pastry (see page 55)

For the filling and decoration

3 tbsp confectioners' sugar, sifted

1 quantity orange mousseline buttercream (see page 150)

1¾ cups (375g) granulated sugar

½ cup (125ml) fresh orange juice, strained

½ cup (125ml) fresh lemon juice, strained

3 small, thin-skinned oranges

1 tbsp dark rum or 1 tsp orange-flower water

1 Allow the pastry to come back to room temperature. Knead briefly until smooth, roll out, and use to line the prepared pan (see page 56). Prick the bottom all over with a fork and chill for 1 hour. Bake with pie weights (see page 56) in the preheated oven for 10 minutes. Uncover and bake for 10–15 minutes longer. Remove from the oven and let cool.

2 For the filling, beat the confectioners' sugar into the buttercream, then spread it over the bottom of the pastry case. Chill for 1 hour.

3 Put the sugar, orange juice, and lemon juice in a large, deep skillet. Leave over low heat until the sugar has dissolved. Bring to a boil and simmer for 20 minutes.

4 Score the skin of the oranges from the stem end to the navel with a small sharp knife. Cut across into ⅛in (2.5mm) thick slices. Lower into the syrup and simmer for 20–30 minutes, or until tender. Lift the slices onto a wire rack and drain for 1 hour.

5 Boil the syrup until reduced and thickened. Stir in the rum or flower water and let cool. Arrange the orange slices over the buttercream and spoon over a thin layer of syrup. Remove from the pan to serve.

 Oven temperature
400°F/200°C

 Baking time
20–25 minutes for the flan case

 Tart pan
9in (23cm) fluted tart pan, greased

 Makes
8–10 slices

 Storage
Keeps for 1 week

 Step ahead
Make the pastry and chill for 1 hour; make the orange mousseline buttercream

Fresh Fig Flan

One summer some years ago we stayed with friends on their farm in Tuscany. The neighbors were away and had asked us to tend their garden, and as a reward we could help ourselves to its produce. The fig trees were laden with luscious, purple fruit that simply had to be eaten. This delicious flan reminds me of that hot, golden summer.

INGREDIENTS

For the flan case

1 quantity pâte sablée pastry (see page 55)

For the filling

½ cup (60g) ground almonds

½ cup (60g) confectioners' sugar

4 tbsp unsalted butter, softened

1 egg

1 tsp finely grated lemon zest

1 pint (375g) fresh figs, halved

3 tbsp simple sugar syrup (see page 153)

1 tbsp fresh lemon juice, strained

confectioners' sugar to decorate

1 Allow the pastry to come back to room temperature. Knead briefly until smooth, roll out, and use to line the prepared pan (see page 56). Prick the bottom all over with a fork and chill for 1 hour. Bake with pie weights (see page 56) in the preheated oven for 10 minutes. Uncover and bake for 10 minutes longer. Remove from the oven and let cool. Reduce the oven temperature.

2 For the filling, beat together the almonds, sugar, butter, egg, and lemon zest until smooth. Spread evenly over the bottom of the pastry case. Lay the figs, cut side up, on top of the filling.

3 Mix the sugar syrup with the lemon juice. Spoon over the figs and bake for 35–45 minutes. Remove from the oven and cool on a wire rack. Take out of the pan and dust with confectioners' sugar to decorate.

 Oven temperature
400°F/200°C, for the flan case; 375°F/190°C for the filling

 Baking time
20 minutes for the flan case; 35–45 minutes for the filling

 Tart pan
9in (23cm) fluted tart pan, greased

 Makes
8–10 slices

 Storage
Best eaten the day it is made

 Step ahead
Make the pastry and chill for 1 hour; make the simple sugar syrup

Pecan & Maple Pie

A great classic from my good friend Nancy Greer, this is her pièce de résistance at dinner parties. Pecans and maple syrup blended in a pie make an irresistible combination that always delights guests.

INGREDIENTS

For the flan case

1 quantity pâte brisée pastry (see page 54)

For the filling

6 tbsp (90g) butter

½ cup (125g) light brown sugar

3 eggs

⅓ cup (100ml) maple syrup

⅔ cup (150ml) golden syrup

1 tbsp Kentucky bourbon or dark rum

pinch of salt

1¼ cups (150g) pecans, coarsely chopped

1 tbsp all-purpose flour

2 cups (250g) pecan halves to decorate

1 Allow the pastry to come back to room temperature. Knead briefly until smooth, roll out on a lightly floured surface, and use to line the prepared pan (see page 56). Chill for 1 hour. Bake with pie weights (see page 56) in the preheated oven for 20 minutes. Remove from the oven, uncover, and lower the temperature.

2 For the filling, beat the butter and sugar together until pale and fluffy. Beat in the eggs, one at a time. Slowly mix in the maple syrup and golden syrup, followed by the bourbon or dark rum and salt.

3 Mix the chopped pecans with the flour and then carefully fold them into the main mixture. Pour into the flan case and bake in the preheated oven for 15 minutes, until the filling is lightly set.

4 Remove the pie from the oven and arrange the pecan halves in concentric circles over the top of the partially set filling. Return to the oven and bake for 30–40 minutes longer, or until completely set; cover with domed foil halfway through if the pie or crust starts to overbrown. Remove from the oven and cool on a wire rack. Take out of the pan and serve warm or cold with cream.

Oven temperature
400°F/200°C for the pastry case; 350°F/180°C for the filling

Baking time
20 minutes for the flan case; 45–55 minutes for the filling

Tart pan
8½ in (22cm), 1½ in (3.5cm) deep, fluted tart pan, greased

Makes
8–10 slices

Storage
Keeps for 3–4 days

Step ahead
Make the pastry and chill for 1 hour

Linzer Torte

This is a delightfully festive jam tart with a distinctive lattice top. It has 18th-century Teutonic origins and remains very popular in North America and throughout Europe. Traditionally, it is made with ground almonds, but modern-day variations often use hazelnuts. Mature for at least one week before serving.

INGREDIENTS

For the pastry

1¼ cups (200g) all-purpose flour
½ tsp ground cinnamon
pinch of ground cloves
14 tbsp (200g) chilled butter, cut into pieces
1½ cups (150g) toasted hazelnuts, finely ground (see page 45)
2 cups (100g) toasted bread crumbs, finely ground (see page 45)
1 cup (200g) granulated sugar
1 egg, lightly beaten
1–2 tbsp dark rum

For the filling and decoration

¾ cup (250g) raspberry or red currant jam, sieved
2 tbsp milk
1 egg yolk, lightly beaten

1 For the pastry, sift the flour and spices together. Add the butter and rub together into a fine crumblike mixture. Stir in the hazelnuts, bread crumbs, and sugar, followed by the egg and rum until the mixture starts to stick together. Knead briefly until smooth. Cut off one third, cover each piece with plastic wrap, and chill for 1 hour.

2 Allow the pastry to come back to room temperature. Roll out the larger piece between waxed paper to a thickness of ¼in (5mm). Use to line the pan (see page 56). Prick all over with a fork and spread with two thirds of the jam.

3 Roll out the remaining pastry and cut into ½in (1cm) wide strips. Arrange over the tart in a lattice design (see page 133), sealing the edge with milk.

4 Brush with the egg yolk and bake in the preheated oven for 30 minutes. Remove from the oven, spoon the remaining jam into each space between the pastry lattice, and let cool.

 Oven temperature
400°F/200°C

 Baking time
30 minutes

 Tart pan
9in (23cm) fluted tart pan, greased

 Makes
8–10 slices

 Storage
Let mature for at least 1 week before serving; keeps for 4–5 weeks

Step ahead
Make the pastry and chill for 1 hour

Fresh Plum Pastry

An unusual sweet and soft German pastry forms the base for my mother's plum cake. The pastry rises between the fruits as it cooks and the slightly tart juices ooze deliciously into the mixture. It can also be made with nectarines, apricots, apples, and other fruit that holds its shape. Dot a little butter over the sugar and cinnamon topping if desired.

INGREDIENTS

For the German pastry

1 cup (125g) self-rising flour
½ cup (125g) chilled butter, cut in pieces
⅓ cup (75g) granulated sugar
1 tsp finely grated lemon zest
1 egg yolk

For the topping

1¼ lb (625g) fresh prune plums, rinsed, cut in half, and pitted
1 tsp ground cinnamon
2 tbsp granulated sugar to decorate

1 For the German pastry, sift the flour into a large bowl, add the butter, and rub together into a fine crumblike mixture. Mix in the sugar and lemon zest. Stir in the egg yolk until everything starts to stick together. Gently squeeze into a ball and knead briefly on a surface lightly dusted with flour until smooth. Cover with plastic wrap and chill for 1 hour.

2 Allow the pastry to come back to room temperature. Knead briefly once more until smooth, then lightly press onto the bottom of the prepared pan. Tightly pack the plums, skin side down, on the pastry but do not press them in. Sprinkle over the cinnamon and 1 tablespoon of the granulated sugar. Bake in the preheated oven for 50 minutes–1 hour, or until the pastry is golden and the fruit is cooked through.

3 Remove the pastry from the oven and let rest for about 5 minutes. Sprinkle the top with the remaining sugar and let cool on a wire rack. Remove from the pan and serve with whipped cream, if you wish.

 Oven temperature
375°F/190°C

Baking time
50 minutes–1 hour

 Cake pan
8½in (22cm) springform pan, greased

 Makes
8 slices

 Storage
Keeps for 2–3 days

❄ **Freezing**
Freezes for 1–2 months

Step ahead
Make the pastry and chill for 1 hour

Tarte Tatin

Who can resist succulent, buttery, caramel-flavored fruit resting on the simplest of shortcrust pastry crusts? The pastry sits on top of the apples during cooking so that when the tart is turned over, the caramelized juices dribble down over the base. (See page 18 for illustration.) It is traditional to make this in a moule à manquer pan, which has a fixed base and sloping sides, so that none of the juices are lost during the cooking process.

INGREDIENTS

For the pastry

1 quantity pâte brisée pastry (see page 54)

For the topping

3lb (1.5kg) small McIntosh apples

6 tbsp (90g) butter

½ cup (100g) granulated sugar

1 Allow the pastry to come back to room temperature. Remove the cores from the apples with an apple corer. Peel and cut them in half.

2 For the topping, put the butter and sugar in a large saucepan or deep skillet. Heat gently until melted. Cook, stirring occasionally, until the mixture starts to caramelize and turns a light brown.

3 Take the pan off the heat and add the apple halves. Gently turn them over in the mixture until well coated, return to high heat, and cook, stirring gently occasionally, for 10 minutes, or until the sauce

has thickened even more and the apples are golden brown.

4 Pack the apples tightly into the bottom of the pan, rounded side down. Roll out the pastry on a lightly floured surface into a circle slightly larger than the top of the pan. Lift carefully onto the apples and tuck the edges down well around the fruit.

5 Bake in the preheated oven for 20 minutes, or until the pastry is golden brown.

6 Remove from the oven and let rest in the pan for 5 minutes so that the juices have time to set slightly; do not leave longer or the caramel sauce and apples will stick to the bottom of the pan and not to the tart.

7 Run a round-bladed knife around the edge of the pastry and carefully invert the tart onto a plate. Let cool slightly. Serve warm with some whipped cream.

 Oven temperature
425°F/220°C

 Baking time
20 minutes

 Cake pan
9½in (24cm) moule à manquer pan or heavy-bottomed, shallow, round cake pan

 Makes
8 slices

 Storage
Best eaten as soon as it is made

 Step ahead
Make the pastry and chill for 1 hour

Tarte au Citron

If you are fond of citrus fruit, then this is an especially fine tart to make. The rich and creamy filling with its sharp lemon tang is complemented by fine-textured, light, crispy pastry. Variations of this French classic are to be found in every chef pâtissier's repertoire. It tastes its best when still slightly warm from the oven.

INGREDIENTS

For the flan case

1 quantity pâte sablée pastry (see page 55)

For the filling

3 eggs

½ cup (125g) granulated sugar

2 tsp finely grated lemon zest

juice of 2 lemons

½ cup (100ml) heavy cream

confectioners' sugar to decorate

1 Allow the pastry to come back to room temperature. Knead briefly until smooth, roll out, and use to line the prepared pan (see page 56). Prick the bottom all over with a fork and chill for 1 hour. Bake with pie weights (see page 56) in the

preheated oven for 10 minutes. Uncover and return to the oven for 10–15 minutes longer.

2 For the filling, lightly mix the eggs and sugar together until pale and creamy but not frothy. Stir in the lemon zest and juice. Fold in the cream and skim off any bubbles.

3 Remove the flan case from the oven and lower the oven temperature. Pour the filling straight into the hot case; this helps it to set and make a seal. Return to the oven and bake for 30 minutes, or until set. Remove from the oven and let cool on a wire rack. Take out of the pan and dust with confectioners' sugar just before serving.

 Oven temperature
400°F/200°C
for the flan case;
250°F/120°C
for the filling

 Baking time
20–25 minutes for the flan case;
30 minutes for the filling

 Tart pan
Shallow 9in (23cm) fluted tart pan, greased

 Makes
8 slices

 Storage
Best eaten as soon as it is made

Fruit & Spice Cakes

Figs, dates, and grapes, ripened in the sun and dried in hot sand, were a staple in the early Mideastern diet and eventually spread worldwide. Spices were imported from the Orient and so highly valued that demand for them caused centuries of warfare. In Arabia, fruit and spices were wrapped in pastry, and in northern Europe they were kneaded into bread doughs. In time, eggs, sugar, butter, and alcohol were introduced to the mixture to create rich fruit cakes.

THE CAKE IS MOIST *and rich in flavor, packed full of apricots, raisins, glacé cherries, and pineapple.*

Brandied Fruit Cake

Special Ingredients

Pecans *give an attractive crunch to the cake's topping.*

Dried apricots and raisins *are softened by boiling with sugar and butter. This also intensifies their flavor.*

Glacé fruit *adds good color and flavor to both the cake mixture and the decorative topping.*

Lemon zest *is the sharply aromatic outer layer of the fruit's skin.*

Brandy *adds a distinctive mellow warmth to the flavor of the cake.*

Marmalade *gives the cake a sharp, fruity tang to balance the sweet glacé fruit.*

Making the Cake

Give this easy cake an alcoholic kick with a weekly "feeding" of two tablespoons of brandy, for two to three weeks (see page 99); then decorate.

INGREDIENTS

For the cake

| 3 cups (375g) all-purpose flour |
| 1 tbsp baking powder |
| 1¾ cups (400ml) water |
| ¾ cup (180g) butter, cut into pieces |
| 1½ cups (375g) granulated sugar |
| ¾ cup (180g) dried apricots, quartered |
| 2 cups (375g) golden raisins |
| ½ cup (125g) glacé cherries, washed, dried, and halved |
| ¼ cup (60g) glacé pineapple, diced |
| 6 tbsp (90ml) brandy |
| 3 eggs, lightly beaten |
| finely grated zest of 1 orange |
| finely grated zest of 1 lemon |

For the decoration

| 4 tbsp sieved orange marmalade |
| ¼ cup (60g) natural glacé cherries, halved |
| ¼ cup (60g) red glacé cherries, halved |
| ½ cup (125g) glacé or crystallized pineapple pieces, halved if thick |
| 1 cup (125g) pecans |
| ¼ cup (60g) angelica, washed, dried, and cut into diamonds |

1 For the cake, sift the flour and baking powder together twice. Set aside. Put the water, butter, sugar, apricots, and raisins in a pan. Slowly bring to a boil over low heat, then boil gently for 20 minutes, stirring occasionally. Let cool.

2 Pour the boiled fruit mixture into a large bowl and stir in the glacé cherries, glacé pineapple, and brandy. Beat in the eggs, followed by the orange and lemon zest. Add the flour and beat together until everything is evenly mixed.

3 Pour the mixture into the prepared pan and level the surface. Bake in the preheated oven for 1½–2 hours, or until a skewer inserted into the cake comes out clean. Cover with domed foil during baking if the top starts to overbrown.

4 Remove from the oven and let cool in the pan on a wire rack. Remove from the pan once cold and carefully peel off the lining paper.

5 For the decoration, put the marmalade in a small pan and warm over gentle heat. Brush half over the top of the cake and arrange the glacé fruit, nuts, and angelica in diagonal lines across the top of the cake. Brush with the remaining marmalade to glaze. Let cool before serving.

Oven temperature
325°F/160°C

Baking time
1½–2 hours

Cake pan
8in (20cm) deep, square pan, greased and double-lined with baking parchment

Makes
24 slices

Storage
Keeps for
1–2 weeks

Freezing
Freezes for 3 months

Simple Ginger Cake

A tasty cake from the northeast of England. It has a strong spicy flavor and the slow cooking produces a moist, sticky texture. Be sure that all the ingredients are at room temperature before you start, and then make the cake using an electric mixer.

INGREDIENTS

- 1¾ cups (250g) self-rising flour
- 1 tsp ground ginger
- ½ cup (125g) light brown sugar
- ¼ cup (175ml) golden syrup
- 2 eggs, lightly beaten
- 5 tbsp (75ml) sunflower or corn oil
- ½ cup (125ml) warm water
- ⅓ cup (90g) ginger marmalade or conserve

1 Sift the flour and ginger together into a bowl. Add the light brown sugar, golden syrup, eggs, oil, water, and marmalade and beat together with an electric mixer until the mixture is pale and thick.

2 Pour the mixture into the prepared pan, place on a baking sheet, and bake in the preheated oven for 2¼ hours, or until a skewer inserted into the cake comes out clean.

3 Remove from the oven, invert onto a wire rack, and carefully peel off the lining paper. Let cool.

Oven temperature
250°F/120°C

Baking time
2¼ hours

Cake pan
9x5x3in (23x12x7cm) loaf pan, greased and lined

Makes
12–15 slices

Storage
Keeps for 5–6 days

Spiced Honey Cake

Christmas honey cakes of northern Europe are usually spiced with cinnamon, ginger, cloves, aniseed, and cardamom and can include almonds instead of rye flour. The mixture is traditionally left to stand for several days to mature and to allow natural leavening to occur. This is a lighter, less spicy cake that is enriched with eggs and sour cream.

INGREDIENTS

For the cake

- ¾ cup (165g) butter
- 1½ cups (325ml) honey
- 4 eggs, separated
- 1¼ cups (165g) all-purpose flour
- 1½ tsp ground cinnamon
- 1½ tsp ground ginger
- 1½ tsp ground cloves
- 1½ tsp baking powder
- 1¼ cups (125g) rye flour
- 1 cup (200ml) sour cream

For the decoration

- 1 quantity lemon glacé icing (see page 152)
- thin slices of crystallized ginger

1 For the cake, melt the butter with the honey. Cool slightly, pour into a bowl, and add the egg yolks. Beat together until pale, thick, and frothy.

2 Sift together the all-purpose flour, spices, and baking powder. Stir in the rye flour. Fold into the egg yolk mixture, followed by the sour cream.

3 Whisk the egg whites into soft peaks. Gently fold into the egg yolk mixture. Pour into the prepared pan and bake in the preheated oven for 20 minutes. Lower the oven temperature and bake for 40–50 minutes.

4 Remove from the oven and let rest for 5 minutes. Invert onto a wire rack, peel off the lining paper, and let cool. Spoon over the icing, decorate with the ginger, and let set.

Oven temperature
325°F/160°C, then 250°F/120°C

Baking time
1 hour–1 hour 10 minutes

Cake pan
8in (20cm) square pan, greased and lined

Makes
9 large or 16 smaller squares

Storage
Keeps for 1–2 weeks

Freezing
Freezes for 2–3 months, undecorated

Irish Barm Brack

Traditionally, this spiced bread was made with yeast and baked in a round pot over a peat fire. Here is a quick and easy alternative. Serve in slices, spread with butter if you prefer.

INGREDIENTS

1 cup (180g) currants

½ cup (90g) golden raisins

scant 1 cup (200ml) hot Darjeeling tea

½ cup (90g) chopped mixed peel

1⅓ cups (250g) light brown sugar

½ tsp ground cinnamon

½ tsp ground allspice

2 eggs

2 tbsp marmalade

1 tsp finely grated lemon zest

2⅔ cups (400g) self-rising flour, sifted

1 Put the currants and raisins in a bowl and pour over the tea. Cover with plastic wrap and let soak overnight. The next day stir in the mixed peel.

2 Put the sugar and spices in another bowl and beat in the eggs, one at a time. Stir in the marmalade and the lemon zest, followed by alternating spoonfuls of the tea and fruit mixture and the flour, until evenly mixed.

3 Spoon the mixture into the prepared pan and level the surface. Bake in the preheated oven for 1–1¼ hours, or until a skewer inserted into the cake comes out clean.

4 Remove the cake from the oven and let cool in the pan on a wire rack. Remove from the pan once cold and peel off the lining paper.

 Oven temperature
350°F/180°C

 Baking time
1–1¼ hours

 Cake pan
8in (20cm) deep, round pan, greased and lined

 Makes
12 slices

 Storage
Keeps for 1 week

 Freezing
Freezes for 1–2 months

Step ahead
Soak the dried fruit in the tea overnight

Traditional English Plum Cake

For centuries now, the most costly and coveted cake ingredients – crystallized fruit, nuts, and spices – have been made into a rich and dark cake served to mark festivals and celebrations. Lace it with spirits, cover it with marzipan, and finish with decorative icing for a traditional Christmas or wedding cake. (See page 27 for illustration.)

INGREDIENTS

1 cup (125g) dried cranberries

¼ cup (125g) dark raisins

1 cup (180g) golden raisins

1 cup (180g) currants

¼ cup (180g) dried apricots, chopped

scant 1 cup (200ml) dark rum or brandy

1 tbsp finely grated orange zest

2 tbsp orange juice

2¼ cups (300g) all-purpose flour

1 tsp freshly grated nutmeg

1 tsp ground cinnamon

½ tsp ground allspice

1 cup (125g) sliced almonds

1 cup (250g) butter, softened

1¼ cups (250g) light brown sugar

4 large eggs, lightly beaten

1 tbsp milk

4–6 tbsp (60–90ml) extra brandy

1 Put all the dried fruit, rum or brandy, orange zest, and orange juice in a bowl. Mix well, cover with plastic wrap, and let soak in a cool place for 24 hours.

2 The next day, sift the flour and spices together. Stir the sliced almonds and a little of the flour into the soaked fruit.

3 Beat the butter and sugar together until pale and fluffy. Gradually beat in the eggs. Stir in alternating spoonfuls of flour and dried fruit until everything is evenly mixed. Stir in the milk.

4 Spoon the mixture into the prepared pan, level the surface, and make a slight dip in the center. Put onto the prepared baking sheet and bake in the preheated oven for 2½ hours, or until a skewer inserted into the cake comes out clean. Cover with a sheet of aluminum foil halfway through to prevent the cake from overbrowning.

5 Remove from the oven and let cool in the pan on a wire rack. Turn out and peel off the lining paper. Wrap in waxed paper and foil and store in an airtight container. Once a week, for 2–3 weeks, pierce the bottom of the cake with a fine skewer, spoon over 2 tablespoons of extra brandy and rewrap.

 Oven temperature
300°F/150°C

 Baking time
2½ hours

 Cake pans
8in (20cm) deep, round pan, greased and lined, and protected with brown paper (see page 43); flat baking sheet, covered with a few layers of brown paper

 Makes
16 slices

 Storage
Keeps for 3 months

 Freezing
Freezes for 1 year

Step ahead
Soak the dried fruit overnight

Chineser Brot

This is a fruited loaf taken from a 19th-century Austrian cooking book. I'm not sure why it is described as Chinese, but it may be because the dates and figs, with their fine, moist textures, hint at Far Eastern luxuries. (See page 22 for illustration.)

INGREDIENTS

For the cake

5 egg yolks

2 egg whites

¼ cup (60g) granulated sugar

½ cup (60g) unblanched almonds, coarsely ground

1oz (30g) semisweet chocolate, grated

1 tsp ground cinnamon

¼ tsp freshly grated nutmeg

2 dried figs, cut into slivers

¼ cup golden raisins

3–4 dried dates, cut into slivers

¼ cup (25g) blanched almonds, sliced

½ cup (25g) toasted white bread crumbs (see page 45)

For the decoration

½ quantity chocolate glacé icing (see page 152)

1 tbsp chopped blanched pistachio nuts

1 For the cake, whisk the egg yolks and sugar together to the ribbon stage (see page 48).

Mix the ground almonds, chocolate, and spices together. Fold into the egg yolk mixture, followed by the dried fruit, sliced almonds, and bread crumbs.

2 In another bowl, whisk the egg whites into soft peaks (see page 47). Stir 2 large spoonfuls into the main mixture to loosen the texture, then gently fold in the remainder.

3 Pour the mixture into the prepared pan and bake in the preheated oven for 25–30 minutes, or until a skewer comes out clean. Remove from the oven and let cool on a wire rack. Take out of the pan and refrigerate for two days before icing.

TO FINISH THE CAKE
Place the cake flat side down, on a wire rack. Pour over the icing (see page 142), sprinkle with the chopped nuts, and let set.

Oven temperature
350°F/180°C

Baking time
25–30 minutes

Cake pan
10½ x 4½ in (27x11cm)
Balmoral or semi-circular pan, greased and floured

Makes
14 slices

Storage
Refrigerate for 2 days before icing; keeps for 2 days once decorated

Freezing
Freezes for 1–2 months, undecorated

Bischofs Brot

In 19th-century northern Europe, a mulled red wine spiced with citrus peel, cinnamon, and cloves, and known as a "Bischof," was often served at dances. The fine, spiced, nutty flavor of this loaf complements the drink very well.

INGREDIENTS

5 eggs, separated

⅔ cup (150g) granulated sugar

½ cup (75g) raisins

2 tbsp pine nuts, coarsely chopped

2 tbsp blanched pistachio nuts, coarsely chopped

¼ cup (45g) blanched, slivered almonds

1 tsp finely grated lemon zest

1 tsp ground cinnamon

½ tsp allspice

¾ cup (100g) all-purpose flour

2 tbsp sliced almonds

1 Whisk the egg yolks and granulated sugar to the ribbon stage (see page 48). Stir in the raisins, chopped pine nuts and pistachio nuts, slivered almonds, and lemon zest.

2 Sift the cinnamon, allspice, and flour together. Stir into

the egg yolk mixture until everything is evenly mixed.

3 In another bowl, whisk the egg whites into soft peaks (see page 47). Stir 2 large spoonfuls into the main mixture to loosen the texture, then gently fold in the remainder.

4 Spoon the mixture into the prepared pan and lightly level the surface. Sprinkle with the sliced almonds. Bake in the center of the preheated oven for 50 minutes, or until a skewer inserted into the middle of the cake comes out clean.

5 Remove the cake from the oven and let it cool in the pan on a wire rack. Remove from the pan and peel off the lining paper. Let stand for two days to allow the flavors to mature before serving.

Oven temperature
325°F/160°C

Baking time
50 minutes

Cake pan
9x5x3in (23x14.5x6.5cm) loaf pan, greased and lined

Makes
15 slices

Storage
Let mature for 2 days before serving; keeps for 1 week

Apricot & Pecan Tea Loaf

With a light, nutty crunch and a distinctive orange tang, this apricot-filled loaf is delicious served just as it is. (See page 22 for illustration.)

INGREDIENTS

For the cake

1 cup (200g) dried apricots
½ cup (75g) pecans, chopped
1⅔ cups (250g) all-purpose flour
¼ tsp salt
½ tsp baking soda
scant ½ cup (100ml) milk
7 tbsp (100g) butter
scant 1 cup (200g) granulated sugar
2 large eggs, lightly beaten
finely grated zest of 1 large orange
½ tsp orange-flower water

For the syrup

2 tbsp orange juice
2 tbsp granulated sugar
pecans and coarse strands of orange zest (see page 149) to decorate

1 Cover the apricots with cold water and let soak overnight.

2 Drain, dry, and chop the apricots. Mix with the nuts and a little of the flour. Sift the rest of the flour with the salt. Blend the baking soda and milk.

3 Beat the butter and sugar together until pale and fluffy. Beat in the eggs, followed by two thirds of the orange zest and the orange-flower water. Gently fold in alternating spoonfuls of flour, milk, and apricot mixture until everything is evenly mixed.

4 Spoon the mixture into the prepared pan and bake in the preheated oven for 1¼ hours, or until a skewer inserted into the cake comes out clean.

5 For the syrup, gently heat the orange juice, sugar, and remaining orange zest in a small heavy-bottomed pan until the sugar has dissolved. Keep warm.

6 Remove the cake from the oven and prick the top all over with a fine skewer. Spoon over the hot syrup and let stand for 10 minutes. Invert onto a wire rack, peel off the lining paper, and let cool. Decorate with the pecans and strands of orange zest.

  Oven temperature
325°F/160°C

 Baking time
1¼ hours

 Cake pan
6¾ x 4½ x 2¼ in (17x11x5.5cm) loaf pan, greased and lined

 Makes
16–20 slices

 Storage
Keeps for 3 weeks

 Freezing
Freezes for 1–2 months

Step ahead
Soak the apricots overnight

Farmhouse Fruit Cake

An English teatime treat from the west country, this traditional, lightly fruited cake is reminiscent of days when the whole family sat down together for high tea after the day's hard work was done. (See page 25 for illustration.)

INGREDIENTS

2½ cups (375g) all-purpose flour
2 tsp baking powder
½ tsp baking soda
½ cup (125g) butter, cut into pieces
½ cup (125g) granulated sugar
6 tbsp (90ml) golden syrup, warmed
2 eggs, lightly beaten
1 cup (250ml) milk
¾ cup (125g) currants
¾ cup (125g) golden raisins
¾ cup (125g) chopped mixed peel
1 tsp finely grated lemon zest
granulated sugar to decorate

1 Sift the flour, baking powder, and baking soda together in a large bowl. Add the butter and cut together into a coarse, crumblike mixture. Stir in the granulated sugar.

2 Pour the golden syrup into another bowl. Add the beaten eggs and milk and whisk together well. Stir into the flour mixture together with the dried fruit, mixed peel, and grated lemon zest until evenly mixed.

3 Pour the mixture into the prepared pan and bake in the preheated oven for 1½ hours, or until a skewer inserted into the cake comes out clean. Remove from the oven, sprinkle with granulated sugar, and let cool in the pan on a wire rack. Turn out, peel off the lining paper, and sprinkle with a little more sugar to decorate.

 Oven temperature
325°F/160°C

 Baking time
1½ hours

 Cake pan
8in (20cm) springform pan, greased and lined

 Makes
8 slices

 Storage
Keeps for 1 week

 Freezing
Freezes for 2–3 months

Nut & Seed Cakes

In Europe there is a passion for cakes filled with nuts and seeds. Such cakes need little enrichment; eggs and sugar almost suffice. Flour is rarely added and butter is often omitted as nuts and seeds contain natural oils that impart a fine moist texture, and it is the separated egg whites whipped into a stiff foam that lighten and give the mixture air. These cakes tend not to rise much but their flavor is strong, pure, and very distinctive.

CHOPPED WALNUTS *in the mixture keep the cake moist.*

POLISH COFFEE AND WALNUT CAKE
A hint of cocoa adds depth of flavor to this classic cake.

Polish Coffee & Walnut Cake

Maria Wosiek, my Polish friend, helped me take care of my sons when they were young; she was always patient and loving, even when they were very naughty. When we went on vacation she would cook special Polish dishes – borscht, stuffed cabbage, "pierozki," and apple fritters. This was her favorite cake.

INGREDIENTS

For the cake

1 tbsp cocoa powder

4 eggs, separated

scant 1 cup (100g) confectioners' sugar

1 tbsp toasted bread crumbs, finely ground (see page 45)

1 tbsp coffee-flavored syrup (see page 153)

1½ cups (180g) walnuts, finely chopped

For the filling and decoration

½ quantity coffee mousseline buttercream (see page 150)

3 tbsp apricot glaze (see page 149)

1 quantity coffee glacé icing (see page 152)

13 walnut halves

chocolate coffee beans

¼ cup (30g) chopped walnuts

1 For the cake, blend the cocoa with 1 teaspoon boiling water. Whisk the egg yolks and sugar together in a bowl to the ribbon stage (see page 48).

2 Gently fold the cocoa, bread crumbs, coffee-flavored syrup, and walnuts into the egg yolk mixture until evenly mixed.

3 In another bowl, whisk the egg whites into soft peaks. Gently fold into the main mixture, taking care not to deflate the whites.

4 Pour the mixture into the prepared pan and bake in the preheated oven for 1 hour. Remove from the oven and let rest for 5 minutes. Invert onto a wire rack and let cool.

5 Slice the cake horizontally in half. Sandwich together with the coffee buttercream. Place on a wire rack set over a plate. Brush all over with apricot glaze, then pour on the glacé icing and coax over the top and sides (see page 142). Decorate with the nut halves, coffee beans, and chopped nuts. Let set before serving.

 Oven temperature
350°F/180°C

 Baking time
1 hour

 Cake pan
8½in (22cm) springform pan, greased and floured

 Makes
12 slices

Storage
Keeps for 3–4 days

❄ **Freezing**
Freezes for 1–2 months, undecorated

Step ahead
Prepare the toasted bread crumbs; make the coffee-flavored syrup and coffee mousseline buttercream

Engadiner Nusstorte

INGREDIENTS

For the pastry

2 quantities German pastry (see page 94), made with all-purpose flour

For the filling

scant 1 cup (200g) granulated sugar

2 cups (250g) walnuts, coarsely chopped

1 cup (250ml) heavy cream

4 tbsp honey, warmed

1 tsp finely grated lemon zest

1 egg white, lightly beaten

1 Make the German pastry (see page 94) and set aside just over half. Roll out the remainder between two sheets of waxed paper into an 8in (20cm) circle. Slide onto a baking sheet and chill until firm. Press the remaining pastry onto the base and up the sides of the prepared pan, using the back of a spoon. Chill until needed.

2 For the filling, put the sugar in a large, heavy-bottomed skillet and heat gently, without stirring, until it has melted and become a pale golden liquid. Immediately take it off the heat and stir in the walnuts. Mix in the cream, honey, and lemon zest. Let cool.

3 Spoon the filling into the pastry case and level the top. Peel the paper off the chilled pastry and lay over the filling. Press the edges together well to seal. Prick the top with a fork and brush with the egg white.

4 Bake in the preheated oven for 25–30 minutes, until golden. Remove from the oven and let cool in the pan on a wire rack. Carefully lift out of the pan and cut into very thin slices to serve.

 Oven temperature
400°F/200°C

Baking time
25–30 minutes

Cake pan
8½in (22cm) springform pan, greased and lined

Makes
12–16 slices

Storage
Keeps for 1–2 weeks

❄ **Freezing**
Freezes for 2–3 months

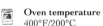

Poppy Seed Strudel

Poppy seed pastries feature strongly in the Christmas baking traditions of Hungary, Austria, Germany, and Poland, and each country has its own variations. Pound the poppy seeds coarsely in a mortar, or grind in an electric coffee grinder, before using. However, take care not to grind them too finely or the oils will be released, making the seeds greasy and bitter tasting.

INGREDIENTS

For the pastry

1 cup (125g) all-purpose flour, sifted
1 cup (125g) self-rising flour, sifted
10 tbsp (150g) butter, cut into pieces
¼ cup (60g) granulated sugar
¼ cup (30g) confectioners' sugar, sifted
1 tsp finely grated lemon zest
1 egg, lightly beaten

For the filling

1 cup (125g) poppy seeds
½ cup (125ml) honey
2 tbsp butter
¾ cup (90g) walnuts, finely chopped
½ cup (90g) raisins

For the decoration

1 egg white, lightly beaten
2 tsp granulated sugar
confectioners' sugar

1 Make the pastry following the method for pâte sucrée (see page 55). Chill for 1 hour.

2 For the filling, coarsely grind the poppy seeds in a clean electric coffee grinder. Put the honey and butter in a pan and melt over low heat. Stir in the poppy seeds, walnuts, and raisins and cook for 1 minute. Let cool slightly.

3 Allow the pastry to come back to room temperature. Knead briefly until smooth. Roll out on a lightly floured surface into a 14x10in (35x25cm) rectangle. Spread over the warm filling to within 1in (2.5cm) of the edge. Roll up from one long edge and pinch the ends together to seal.

4 Lay the roll on the prepared baking sheet, seamside down, brush with the egg white, and sprinkle with the sugar. Bake in the preheated oven for 25–30 minutes, or until golden.

5 Remove from the oven and let rest for 5 minutes. Move to a wire rack and let cool. Dust with confectioners' sugar and cut into thin slices once cold.

Oven temperature
375°F/190°C

Baking time
25–30 minutes

Cake pan
14x10in (35x25cm) cookie sheet, greased with butter

Makes
20 slices

Storage
Keeps for 1 week

Step ahead
Make the pastry and chill for 1 hour

Nun's Seed Cake

Here is a recipe for caraway seed cake adapted from Hannah Glasse's The Art of Cookery Made Plain & Easy, written in 1747. I was delighted to discover that the flavors of caraway and orange-flower water enhance each other.

INGREDIENTS

1¼ cups (200g) self-rising flour
1 tsp ground cinnamon
scant 1 cup (200g) butter
⅔ cup (150g) granulated sugar
3 eggs
2 tsp orange-flower or rose water
2–3 tsp caraway seeds

1 Sift the flour and cinnamon together twice in a bowl and set aside.

2 In another bowl, beat the butter until soft and creamy. Add the granulated sugar and beat together for 3–4 minutes, until pale and fluffy.

3 Beat in the eggs, one at a time, adding a little of the sifted flour and cinnamon with the last egg if the mixture begins to separate.

4 Carefully fold the remaining flour into the main mixture, followed by the orange-flower water or rose water and the caraway seeds, until everything is evenly mixed.

5 Spoon the mixture into the prepared pan and lightly level the surface. Bake in the preheated oven for 45 minutes– 1 hour, or until richly golden and a skewer inserted into the cake comes out clean.

6 Remove from the oven and let rest in the pan for about 10 minutes. Invert onto a wire rack and let cool.

Oven temperature
350°F/180°C

Baking time
45 minutes–1 hour

Cake pan
9x5x3in (23x14.5x6.5cm) loaf pan, greased and lined

Makes
16 slices

Storage
Keeps for 4–5 days

Freezing
Freezes for 1–2 months

Hazelnut Cake

Passover, or Pesach, commemorates the exodus of the Jews from Egypt during the rule of the Pharaohs. By Jewish law, it is forbidden to eat any baked goods containing leavening agents or flour, so cakes made with nuts are popular. The texture of this cake is light yet deliciously nutty, and it has a distinctive orange flavor. It tastes even better covered in a layer of melted semisweet chocolate (see step 4 for the Whipped Almond Cake below).

INGREDIENTS

¾ cup (180g) granulated sugar

4 eggs, separated

1 tbsp cocoa powder

1 tbsp finely grated orange zest

1¼ cups (200g) toasted hazelnuts, finely chopped (see page 45)

3 tbsp matzo meal or toasted white bread crumbs (not for Passover), finely ground (see page 45)

2 tsp orange juice

confectioners' sugar to decorate

1 Set aside 4 tablespoons of the sugar. Whisk the remainder with the egg yolks and cocoa powder to the ribbon stage (see page 48). Whisk in the zest.

2 In another bowl, whisk the egg whites into soft peaks. Whisk in the reserved sugar to form slightly stiffer peaks (see page 49). Stir 2 large spoonfuls of the egg whites into the egg yolk mixture to loosen the texture slightly.

3 Mix together the hazelnuts and matzo meal or toasted bread crumbs. Fold into the egg yolk mixture. Gently fold in the remaining egg whites taking care not to deflate them. Fold in the orange juice.

4 Spoon the mixture into the prepared pan and lightly level the surface. Bake in the preheated oven for 55 minutes, or until a skewer inserted into the cake comes out clean. Cover with a domed piece of foil toward the end of the cooking time if it starts to overbrown.

5 Remove from the oven and let rest for 10 minutes. Invert onto a wire rack and let cool. Peel off the lining paper. Dust with confectioners' sugar and serve with whipped cream.

 Oven temperature
350°F/180°C

 Baking time
55 minutes

 Cake pan
8½in (22cm) springform pan, greased and lined

 Makes
12 slices

Storage
Keeps for 1 week

Freezing
Freezes for 1–2 months

Step ahead
Prepare the toasted hazelnuts, and toasted bread crumbs if using

Whipped Almond Cake

This cake is very quick and easy to prepare, and also suitable for Passover. It contains no flour: air is the only leavening agent, so be sure to whisk the mixture well and then fold in the almonds and egg whites swiftly but gently. This is used as a delicious base sponge in the Esterházy Cream Torte (see page 71).

INGREDIENTS

For the cake

6 eggs

⅔ cup (150g) granulated sugar

1 tsp finely grated orange zest

1¼ cups (150g) ground almonds

For the decoration

4 tbsp apricot glaze (see page 149)

7oz (200g) semisweet chocolate

1 For the cake, separate 4 of the eggs and set aside 2 tablespoons of the granulated sugar. Whisk the remaining sugar with the egg yolks, whole eggs, and orange zest to the ribbon stage (see page 48). Gradually stir in the ground almonds, until evenly mixed.

2 In another bowl, whisk the egg whites into soft peaks. Whisk in the reserved sugar to form slightly stiffer peaks (see page 49). Gently fold into the main mixture, taking care not to deflate the whites.

3 Pour the mixture into the prepared pan and bake in the preheated oven for 1 hour, or until a skewer inserted into the cake comes out clean. Remove from the oven and let rest for 5 minutes. Invert onto a wire rack and peel off the lining paper.

4 Place the cake, right side up, on a wire rack set over a plate. Brush the top and sides with the apricot glaze. Melt the chocolate (see page 44), then cool slightly until thickened but not set. While still warm, pour the chocolate onto the center of the cake and spread evenly over the top and sides with a small narrow spatula (see page 142). Let set before serving.

 Oven temperature
325°F/160°C

 Baking time
1 hour

 Cake pan
9in (23cm) springform pan, greased and lined

 Makes
12 slices

 Storage
Keeps for 1 week

 Freezing
Freezes for 1–2 months, undecorated

 Step ahead
Make the apricot glaze

Coconut Layer Cake

Coconut cakes are often very sweet and heavy. I include sour cream, which helps lighten the cake, makes it fluffier, and brings out its distinct coconut taste. The fresh flavor of the strawberry jelly filling complements the cake well, particularly when it is accompanied by a sweet cream cheese frosting. If you have not used a fresh coconut before, the steps below show you how to extract the milk and the flesh. (See page 23 for illustration.)

INGREDIENTS

For the cake

2 cups (180g) finely grated fresh coconut (see below)

¾ cup (180g) butter

1⅔ cups (375g) granulated sugar

3 eggs

1½ cups (300ml) sour cream

1¼ cups (200g) self-rising flour, sifted

½ cup (125ml) fresh coconut milk

For the filling and decoration

1 cup (150ml) strawberry jelly

6oz (180g) cream cheese

½ cup (125g) unsalted butter, softened

½ tsp vanilla extract

4 cups (500g) confectioners' sugar, sifted

toasted coconut shavings (see below)

1 For the cake, set aside ¾ cup (75g) of the grated coconut. Spread the remainder on a baking sheet and bake in the preheated oven for 15 minutes, stirring every now and then, until it is dry and lightly golden. Let cool.

2 Beat the butter and sugar together until pale and fluffy. Beat in the eggs, one at a time. Gently stir in the sour cream, followed by the flour, the fresh coconut milk, and the toasted coconut until evenly mixed.

3 Spoon the mixture into the prepared pans and bake in the preheated oven for 35 minutes, or until a skewer inserted into each cake comes out clean. Remove from the oven and let rest in the pans for 10 minutes. Invert onto a wire rack, carefully peel off the lining paper, and let cool.

TO FINISH THE CAKE

1 Slice each cake horizontally in half. Sandwich each one back together with the strawberry jelly.

2 For the frosting, beat the cream cheese, butter, and vanilla extract together until smooth. Gradually beat in the confectioners' sugar. Sandwich the two cakes together with 5–6 tablespoons of the frosting.

3 Spread the remaining cream cheese frosting evenly over the top and sides of the cake, then coat with the reserved grated fresh coconut (see page 143). Decorate the top of the cake with the toasted coconut shavings (see steps 3–4 below).

Oven temperature
350°F/180°C

Baking time
35 minutes

Cake pans
Two 8½in (22cm) round cake pans, greased and lined

Makes
12 slices

Storage
Keeps for 2–3 days in the refrigerator

❄ **Freezing**
Freezes for 1–2 months, undecorated

Step ahead
Prepare the fresh coconut and the toasted shavings (see steps 1–4 below)

Preparing a Fresh Coconut

1 Pierce two of the eyes with a skewer. Drain the milk through a cheesecloth-lined sieve into a cup. Bake the coconut at 325°F/160°C for 20 minutes.

2 Remove the coconut from the oven and cool slightly. Then wrap in a cloth and sharply tap the shell with a small hammer. It will crack open quite easily.

3 Separate the husk from the flesh and discard it. Peel the brown skin off most of the flesh with a vegetable peeler and finely grate for the cake.

4 Peel the remaining flesh into long, thin strips with a vegetable peeler. Spread on a baking sheet and toast under the broiler for 3–4 minutes.

Spanish Almond Sponge

Almonds, honey, and sugar are extremely popular ingredients in Spanish cakes and candies. Originating in early convent kitchens for the celebration of Christmas, such cakes are now eaten throughout the year. Brush the top of the cake with a little warmed honey before decorating with the sliced almonds and confectioners' sugar if you wish.

INGREDIENTS

For the cake

5 tbsp (75g) butter

¾ cup (180g) granulated sugar

1 tsp finely grated orange zest

2 eggs, lightly beaten

¾ cup (90g) all-purpose flour, sifted

¾ cup (90g) ground almonds

2 tsp brandy or Grand Marnier

¼ cup (30g) sliced almonds

For the filling

½ cup (150ml) heavy cream

2 tbsp granulated sugar

1 tbsp brandy or Grand Marnier

¼ cup (45g) toasted sliced almonds

For the decoration

¼ cup (30g) toasted sliced almonds

confectioners' sugar

1 Beat the butter, sugar, and orange zest together until pale and fluffy. Gradually beat in the eggs. Fold in alternating spoonfuls of flour and ground almonds until everything is evenly mixed. Fold in the brandy or Grand Marnier.

2 Pour the mixture into the prepared pan, sprinkle with the sliced almonds, and bake in the preheated oven for about 40 minutes, or until a skewer inserted into the cake comes out clean. Remove from the oven and let rest in the pan for 5 minutes. Invert onto a wire rack and let cool.

3 For the filling, whip the cream, sugar, and brandy or Grand Marnier into soft peaks. Fold in the toasted almonds.

4 Slice the cake horizontally in half. Sandwich the layers together with the almond cream filling and transfer to a plate. Sprinkle the top of the cake with the remaining toasted sliced almonds, then dust lightly with confectioners' sugar to decorate.

  Oven temperature
350°F/180°C

 Baking time
40 minutes

 Cake pan
8in (20cm) springform pan, greased and floured

 Makes
8 slices

 Storage
Keeps for 2–3 days

❄ **Freezing**
Freezes for 1–2 months

Cheesecakes

Traditionally made for festive occasions, the first cheesecakes were simply soft cheeses perfumed with spices and flower waters, then wrapped in thin pastry cases and baked. Today baked cheesecakes are gloriously rich and made from farmer or cream cheeses, eggs, sugar, and flavorings. They should be dense without being cloying. Contemporary cheesecakes can also be fruity, cold-set, and refreshingly light confections.

Mango & Passion Fruit Cheesecake

This chilled cheesecake makes a stunning dinner-party dessert. The fruit gives both tempting color and intense and aromatic flavor to counterbalance the richness of the Italian soft cheese.

Special Ingredients

Fresh mango

Kiwi fruit

Passion fruit

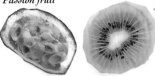

Mango, passion fruit, and kiwi fruit add color and flavor to this fresh fruited cheesecake.

Graham crackers make a delicious base for cheesecakes and are easy to crush in a sealed plastic bag.

Ground cinnamon gives subtle flavor to the cracker base, and complements the flavor of the mango perfectly.

Nutmeg adds a warm spicy note. Grate it fresh for the recipe just before using.

Apricot jam subtly flavors and helps to bind the cracker crumb base.

Gelatin is sprinkled onto cold liquid, then gently heated until clear. It lightly sets the rich cheese filling.

Making the cheesecake

The lightly spiced, crushed-cracker base contrasts well with the creamy smooth topping, exotically flavored with refreshing passion fruit juice and pieces of mango.

INGREDIENTS

For the base

3 cups (180g) crushed graham crackers
½ tsp ground cinnamon
pinch of freshly grated nutmeg
5 tbsp (75g) butter
1 tbsp apricot jam

For the filling

14oz (425g) canned or frozen mango slices
1½ tbsp unflavored gelatin
6 passion fruit
grated zest and juice of 1 orange
4 eggs, separated
⅔ cup (150g) granulated sugar
1 cup (200g) mascarpone cheese
1 cup (250ml) heavy cream, whipped

For the decoration

2 fresh mangoes, peeled and sliced
1–2 kiwi fruit, peeled and sliced
pulp from 1 passion fruit

1 For the base, mix the crackers and spices together. Melt the butter and the apricot jam. Mix into the crackers and then spoon into the prepared pan. Press evenly onto the bottom with a spoon, then chill.

2 For the filling, drain the canned mangoes and spoon 6 tablespoons (90ml) of the juice into a heatproof bowl. Sprinkle with the gelatin and let stand for 5 minutes. Sit the bowl in a pan of simmering water and let stand until clear (see page 45). Remove and set aside.

3 Decorate the sides of the prepared pan with 5–6 of the mango slices. Roughly chop the remainder. Halve the passion fruit, scoop the pulp into a sieve, and press the juice into a bowl. Stir the orange zest and juice into the passion fruit juice with the chopped mango and dissolved gelatin.

4 Whisk the egg yolks and sugar together until thick and mousselike. Whisk in the mascarpone cheese. Stir in the fruit mixture and set aside until it starts to thicken and set.

5 Whisk the egg whites into soft peaks (see page 47). Quickly fold the whipped cream into the setting cheese mixture, followed by the egg whites. Pour into the pan and chill for at least 5 hours, or until set.

6 Remove from the pan and transfer to a plate. Decorate the top with the mango and kiwi fruit slices. Spoon the passion fruit pulp into the center.

Cake pan
8½in (22cm) springform pan, greased lightly with vegetable oil and lined

Makes
10–12 slices

Storage
Keeps for 3 days

Warning
This recipe contains raw eggs (see page 9)

16th-Century Maids of Honor

Anne Boleyn, who was a Maid of Honor at the court of King Henry VIII in 1552, and later became one of his ill-fated wives, reputedly baked these cheese tartlets to tempt His Majesty. He seemed to approve, for he named them in her honor. Take care not to overfill the tartlet cases or the mixture will run over the sides as they bake.

INGREDIENTS

For the pastry cases

1 quantity pâte brisée pastry (see page 54)

For the filling

6 tbsp (90g) butter, softened

½ cup (125g) farmer cheese

2 egg yolks

⅓ cup (90g) granulated sugar

1 tsp finely grated lemon zest

½ cup (60g) ground almonds

1 tsp orange-flower water

pinch of freshly grated nutmeg

2 tbsp lemon juice

½ cup (75g) candied peel, finely chopped

1 Allow the pastry to come back to room temperature.

Knead briefly until smooth. Roll out until thin on a lightly floured surface and cut out twenty-four 3in (7cm) circles using a fluted cookie cutter. Press into the prepared muffin tins, prick with a fork, and chill for 20 minutes.

2 For the filling, beat together the butter and farmer cheese until smooth. Beat in the egg yolks, sugar, zest, almonds, and orange-flower water. Stir in the nutmeg and lemon juice.

3 Drop a little candied peel into each pastry case. Spoon in some filling until just over half full. Bake in the preheated oven for 20–25 minutes. Remove from the oven and let cool in the tins.

 Oven temperature
400°F/200°C

 Baking time
20–25 minutes

 Cake pans
Two deep 12-hole muffin tins, greased

 Makes
24 tartlets

 Storage
Keep for 1–2 days

 Freezing
Freeze for 1 month

 Step ahead
Make the pastry and chill for 1 hour

Pêches à la Melba Cheesecake

Dame Nellie Melba, the Australian opera singer, was a regular visitor to London's Savoy Hotel during the 1890s. Auguste Escoffier, the chef at the time, dedicated a dessert of peaches, ice cream, and raspberry purée to the renowned artiste. Here is a further tribute to them both. (See page 17 for illustration.)

INGREDIENTS

For the base

1 quantity pâte sucrée pastry (see page 55)

For the filling

½ cup (60g) ground almonds

1 tbsp granulated sugar

1½ lb (750g) ripe fresh peaches, halved, pitted, and peeled (or use frozen peaches)

10oz (300g) cream cheese

⅓ cup (90ml) sour cream

¼ cup (60g) granulated sugar

3 eggs, separated

1 tsp finely grated lemon zest

For the decoration

10 fresh raspberries

mint sprigs

confectioners' sugar

1 quantity raspberry sauce (see page 149)

1 Allow the pastry to come back to room temperature. Knead briefly until smooth and roll out on a lightly floured surface into a 10in (25cm) circle. Press onto the bottom and slightly up the sides of the prepared pan. Prick all over with a fork and bake with pie weights for 10 minutes

(see page 56). Uncover and bake for 10 minutes more. Remove from the oven and let cool completely. Lower the oven temperature.

2 For the filling, mix together the almonds and sugar and spread evenly over the pastry. Arrange the peach halves on top.

3 Beat the cheese, sour cream, and sugar together until smooth. Mix in the egg yolks and lemon zest. Whisk the egg whites into soft peaks. Stir 2 spoonfuls into the cheese mixture, then gently fold in the remainder.

4 Pour the mixture into the pan and bake for 1¼ hours. Cover with domed foil halfway through baking to prevent overbrowning. Turn off the oven and leave the cake inside until cold.

5 Remove from the pan and decorate with the fresh raspberries and mint. Dust with confectioners' sugar and serve with the raspberry sauce.

 Oven temperature
400°F/200°C
for the base;
325°F/160°C
for the cheesecake

 Baking time
20 minutes for the base; 1¼ hours for the cheesecake

 Cake pan
9½in (24cm) springform pan, greased

 Makes
8–10 slices

 Storage
Keeps for 2–3 days

 Step ahead
Make the pastry and chill for 1 hour; prepare the fresh peaches; make the raspberry sauce

Hoboken Cinnamon Cheesecake

My youngest son, Jeremy, owns "Oddfellow's Rest," a bar and restaurant in Hoboken, New Jersey. This is the most popular cake on the menu. The recipe was given to me by his chef, Wayne Haney.

INGREDIENTS

For the filling

½ cup (75g) raisins
2 tbsp dark rum
2lb (1kg) ricotta cheese
½ cup (125g) granulated sugar
2 tsp cornstarch, sifted
½ tsp vanilla extract
1–2 tbsp ground cinnamon
2 large eggs
2 egg yolks
1 cup (250ml) sour cream

For the base

1 pack or 11 graham crackers, crushed
2 tbsp cocoa powder
½ cup (125g) light brown sugar
4 tbsp butter, melted and cooled
1 small egg white, lightly beaten

1 Soak the raisins in the rum for 30 minutes, then drain.

2 For the base, put the crushed crackers, cocoa, and sugar in a bowl. Stir in the butter and egg white until everything is well mixed. Press evenly onto the bottom of the prepared pan.

3 For the filling, beat the ricotta cheese and sugar together until smooth. Beat in the cornstarch, vanilla, and cinnamon, followed by the whole eggs and egg yolks, one at a time. Dry the raisins well and fold in with the sour cream. Pour into the pan.

4 Bake in the preheated oven for 10 minutes. Lower the oven temperature and bake for 1 hour 40 minutes longer, until set, covering with domed foil if it starts to overbrown. Turn off the oven and let cool inside. Remove from the pan to serve.

Oven temperature
400°F/200°C,
then
300°F/150°C

Baking time
10 minutes at the higher temperature, then 1 hour 40 minutes at the lower temperature

Cake pan
9½in (24cm) springform pan, greased

Makes
10 slices

Storage
Keeps for 2–3 days

Freezing
Freezes for 1–2 months

Golden Baked Cheesecake

A traditional baked cheesecake, this has a rich yet delicate texture. The cake collapses in the center as it cools and sometimes cracks, but don't worry, that's exactly the way it should be. (See page 16 for illustration.)

INGREDIENTS

For the filling

⅓ cup (60g) raisins
2 tbsp dark rum
1½ cups (400g) farmer cheese
½ cup (125ml) sour cream
2 eggs, separated
1 egg yolk
½ cup (125g) granulated sugar
1 tbsp vanilla sugar
2 tsp finely grated lemon zest
confectioners' sugar to decorate

For the base

1 quantity pâte brisée pastry (see page 54)

1 Soak the raisins in the rum overnight in a covered bowl.

2 Allow the pastry to come back to room temperature. Knead briefly until smooth. Roll out half on a lightly floured surface into a 9in (23cm) circle. Press evenly onto the bottom and slightly up the sides of the prepared pan. Prick all over with a fork and bake in the preheated oven for 10–15 minutes. Remove from the oven and let cool. Lower the oven temperature.

3 Roll out the remaining pastry into a 1in (2.5cm) long band. Cut in half lengthwise. Use to line the sides of the pan, pressing them onto the bottom to seal.

4 For the filling, beat the cheese, cream, egg yolks, granulated and vanilla sugars, and zest together until thick. In another bowl, whisk the egg whites into soft peaks (see page 47). Stir 2 spoonfuls into the cheese mixture, then gently fold in the rest. Fold in the raisins.

5 Pour the mixture into the pan and bake for 1 hour. Turn off the oven and let cool inside. Remove from the pan and dust with the sugar to serve.

Oven temperature
400°F/200°C
for the base;
350°F/180°C
for the cheesecake

Baking time
10–15 minutes for the base; 1 hour for the cheesecake

Cake pan
8½in (22cm) springform pan, greased

Makes
10–12 slices

Storage
Keeps for 2–3 days

Freezing
Freezes for 1–2 months

Step ahead
Soak the raisins; make the pastry and chill for 1 hour

Meringues

Egg whites, the simplest of ingredients, are vigorously whisked into an airy froth and then combined with sugar to make a thick and glossy foam, which is shaped and then baked very gently until crisp, dry, and lightly browned. The resulting confection melts in the mouth to a delicious sugary nothingness. It wonderfully complements all the finest cake creams, fruit, and fillings, and blends delectably with nuts. Plain meringues keep well, so if you have some on hand you can produce a tempting dessert in moments.

Simple Meringues

Meringues are easy to make, and when covered with whipped cream and other sumptuous ingredients, such as soft fruit or chocolate, they must surely be an all-time favorite. Remember that eggs should always be at room temperature before starting preparation. Simple meringues can be stored in an airtight container or wrapped in aluminum foil.

INGREDIENTS

2 egg whites

pinch of cream of tartar

½ cup (125g) superfine sugar

chopped nuts or granulated sugar

⅔ cup (150ml) heavy cream, whipped

fresh strawberries to decorate

1 Put the egg whites in a large, clean bowl and whisk slowly until they become thick and frothy. Add the cream of tartar and continue to whisk more quickly until the whites form stiff peaks (see page 49).

2 Sprinkle over half the superfine sugar and continue whisking until the mixture is stiff and glossy. The remaining sugar can be added in one of two ways: either sprinkle it over the meringue, half at a time, and gently fold it in, or, for a firmer meringue that is particularly good for piping (see page 49), whisk in the rest of the sugar a little at a time.

FOR SIMPLE MERINGUES
For individual meringues, scoop out 10 large spoonfuls of the meringue mixture and push them onto the prepared baking sheet, about ¾in (2cm) apart (see page 49). Alternatively, spoon the mixture into a pastry bag fitted with a ½in (1cm) plain or star nozzle and pipe 3in (7cm) mounds onto the baking sheet. Sprinkle with a few chopped, toasted hazelnuts, pistachio nuts, sliced almonds or granulated sugar if you wish.

FOR MERINGUE DISKS
To make a meringue disk, mark the prepared baking sheet with an 8½in (22cm) circle as a guideline. Spoon the mixture onto the baking sheet and spread out within the marked circle to a thickness of about ¾in (2cm). (Remember the meringue will expand during cooking.) Alternatively, spoon the mixture into a pastry bag fitted with a ½in (1cm) plain nozzle and, starting in the center of the marked circle, pipe in a spiral pattern to form a flat disk (see page 49). Sprinkle lightly with a little granulated sugar if wished.

TO COOK THE MERINGUE
Bake in the preheated oven until crisp and dry (see page 49). The time taken will depend on the size of the meringue. Allow 50 minutes–1 hour for individual meringues and 1½–2 hours for a meringue disk. Turn off the oven and leave the meringues inside until completely cold. Lift off the baking parchment.

TO FINISH THE MERINGUE
Sandwich individual meringues together with the whipped cream and decorate with the fresh strawberries.

 Oven temperature
250°F/120°C

 Baking time
50 minutes–1 hour for individual meringues; 1½–2 hours for meringue disks

 Cake pan
One or two flat baking sheets, lined with baking parchment

 Makes
10 individual meringues (5 pairs), or one 8½in (22cm) meringue disk

 Storage
Keep for 1–2 months, unfilled, wrapped in aluminum foil or stored in an airtight container

Special Toppings for Meringue Disks

Cranberry and Orange Meringue

Cook 2 cups (250g) fresh or frozen cranberries with 1 teaspoon grated orange zest, 2 strips orange peel, and ½ cup (125ml) water for 10 minutes. Remove the orange strips. Stir in ½ cup (125g) granulated sugar, then cool. Spread an 8½ in (22cm) meringue disk with 1¼ cups (300ml) whipped heavy cream. Spoon over the cranberries. Decorate with orange shreds.

Chocolate Cream Meringue

Spread an 8½ in (22cm) meringue disk with 1¼ cups (300ml) whipped heavy cream, flavored with 2 tablespoons granulated sugar and 2 tablespoons cointreau or dark rum. Sprinkle with 3½ oz (100g) grated semisweet chocolate.

Autumn Fruit Meringue

Spread an 8½ in (22cm) meringue disk with 1¼ cups (300ml) whipped heavy cream. Sprinkle with 1lb (500g) mixed fruits such as blackberries, loganberries, sliced plums, black grapes, and blueberries.

Chestnut Meringue

Beat together 1¼ cups (300g) unsweetened chestnut purée, ¼ cup (60g) granulated sugar, and 1 tablespoon dark rum. Stir in 4 tablespoons lightly whipped heavy cream. Spoon into a pastry bag fitted with a ¼ in (5mm) plain nozzle. Pipe long strands over the top of an 8½ in (22cm) meringue disk, sprinkle with thin slices of marrons glacés, and dust with confectioners' sugar to decorate.

Summer Berry Vacherin

A meringue vacherin is surely one of the most delightful – and beautiful – desserts imaginable. The light and crisp sugary layers brimming with richly colored berries combined with liqueur-laced fruity cream are quite irresistible. (See page 21 for illustration.)

INGREDIENTS

For the meringues

4 quantities Simple Meringues mixture (see page 112)

granulated sugar

For the filling

½ pint (250ml) fresh raspberries

6 tbsp (90g) granulated sugar

1 pint (500ml) fresh strawberries

5 cups (1.25 liters) heavy cream

6 tbsp (90ml) Grand Marnier

For the decoration

1 cup (90g) fresh blueberries

1 cup (125g) mixed fresh red currants, black currants, and white currants

½ pint (250ml) fresh strawberries, halved

1 kiwi, peeled, sliced, and halved

1 cup (90g) fresh blackberries

1 Mark an 8½ in (22cm) circle on each prepared baking sheet. Make two quantities of the meringue mixture and spread out equally within the marked circles (see page 49).

2 Make another two quantities of the meringue mixture and spoon into a pastry bag fitted with a ½ in (1cm) star nozzle. Pipe a line of 1in (2.5cm) stars around the edge of each disk. On the third disk, pipe a second row of stars over the first.

3 Sprinkle each disk with some granulated sugar. Bake in the preheated oven for 2½ – 3 hours, until crisp and dry. Turn off the oven and let cool inside.

4 For the filling, crush the raspberries with about 2 tablespoons of the sugar. Chop the strawberries and press through a plastic sieve or purée in a blender. Stir in 2 tablespoons of the sugar. Whip the cream, remaining sugar, and Grand Marnier into soft peaks. Mix one third with the crushed raspberries, another third with the puréed strawberries, and leave the remainder plain.

5 Lift the the meringues off the parchment. Put one flat disk on a plate and spread with the raspberry cream. Cover with the second flat disk and spread over the strawberry cream. Cover with the last disk and spoon the plain cream into the center. Arrange the fruit on top and serve within 1–2 hours.

Oven temperature
225°F/110°C

Baking time
2½–3 hours

Cake pans
Three flat baking sheets, lined with baking parchment

Makes
10–12 slices

Storage
The meringue disks keep for 1–2 months, wrapped in aluminum foil or stored in an airtight container; best eaten within 1–2 hours of assembly

Nectarine Pavlova

Anna Pavlova was the famous Russian ballerina for whom "The Dying Swan" was created. This lovely, soft meringue is reputed to have been created in Australia in her honor.

INGREDIENTS

For the meringue

4 egg whites

1¼ cups (250g) superfine sugar

1 tsp vanilla extract

1 tsp white vinegar or lemon juice

2 tsp cornstarch

For the topping

3 nectarines, 2 peaches, and about ½ lb (250g) cherries

2 tbsp vanilla sugar

2¼ cups (450ml) heavy cream

1½ tbsp Grand Marnier

1 Mark a 9in (23cm) circle or oval on the prepared baking sheet. For the meringue, whisk the egg whites into stiff peaks. Gradually whisk in the sugar, 1 tablespoon at a time, until it forms a stiff, glossy meringue (see page 49). Whisk in the vanilla extract, vinegar or lemon juice, and cornstarch.

2 Spoon the mixture onto the prepared baking sheet and spread within the marked circle (see page 49). Make a slight dip in the center of the meringue so that the outside edge is slightly higher. Bake in the preheated oven for 1–1¼ hours, or until lightly browned, hard to the touch on the outside, and marshmallowlike in the center. Turn off the oven and let cool inside. Remove from the oven and carefully lift off the baking parchment.

3 For the topping, halve, pit and slice the nectarines and peaches and pit the cherries. Put into a shallow dish and sprinkle with the vanilla sugar. Whip the heavy cream with the Grand Marnier into soft peaks.

4 Just before serving, spread the cream over the top of the Pavlova and pile the fruit decoratively on top.

VARIATION
Tropical Fruit Pavlova
For the topping, use 1½lb (750g) prepared mixed fresh tropical fruit such as pineapple, kiwi fruit, banana, papaya, and mango. Prepare and assemble following the main recipe above, using granulated, not vanilla, sugar.

 Oven temperature
300°F/160°C

 Baking time
1–1¼ hours

 Cake pan
Flat baking sheet, lined with baking parchment

 Makes
6–8 slices

 Storage
Keeps for 2–3 days, undecorated

Torta di Pignoli

Pine nuts are harvested from the stone pine, which is native to southwest Europe. The nut is commonly used in Arab cuisine and was introduced to Italy by early travelers. Pine nuts can be eaten raw but take on a better flavor when toasted, as in this delicious pine nut cake. They should be used while fresh as they grow rancid after only three or four months. (See page 20 for illustration.)

INGREDIENTS

1⅓ cups (200g) pine nuts

3 egg whites

1 cup (225g) superfine sugar

1 tbsp lemon juice

1⅓ cups (300ml) heavy cream

confectioners' sugar to decorate

1 Spread the pine nuts on a baking sheet and toast in the preheated oven for 4–5 minutes. Cool, then set aside 2 tablespoons of nuts and finely chop the rest. Lower the oven temperature.

2 Mark a 9in (23cm) circle on each prepared baking sheet. Whisk the egg whites into stiff peaks. Gradually whisk in the sugar until it forms a stiff, glossy meringue (see page 49). Gently fold in the chopped pine nuts and lemon juice.

3 Spoon the meringue into a pastry bag fitted with a ½in (1cm) plain nozzle. Pipe a disk onto each prepared baking sheet (see page 49) and bake for 45–50 minutes. Remove from the oven, lift off the parchment, and let cool on a rack.

4 Whip the cream into soft peaks and use to sandwich the two disks. Sprinkle the cake with the reserved pine nuts and confectioners' sugar.

 Oven temperature
350°F/180°C;
then
325°F/160°C

 Baking time
45–50 minutes

 Cake pans
Two flat baking sheets, lined with baking parchment

 Makes
8 slices

 Storage
Keeps for 1–2 days

 Step ahead
Toast the pine nuts

Mocha Tranche

A layer cake with a difference: crisp rectangular layers of mocha-flavored meringue are sandwiched together with coffee-liqueur-flavored cream and decorated with delicious melt-in-the-mouth meringue batons.

INGREDIENTS

For the meringue

2 quantities Simple Meringues mixture (see page 112)
2 tbsp cocoa powder
4 tsp instant coffee

For the filling and decoration

2½ cups (600ml) heavy cream
1 tbsp granulated sugar
2–3 tbsp Tia Maria
cocoa powder

1 Mark three 12 x 4in (30 x 10cm) rectangles on three of the prepared baking sheets.

2 Make the meringue mixture (see page 112). Mix the cocoa and coffee powder together, sift over the meringue mixture, and whisk in until everything is evenly mixed.

3 For the meringue batons, spoon 2 large spoonfuls of the mixture into a pastry bag fitted with a ¼ in (5mm) plain nozzle. Pipe 3in (7.5cm) lines on the unmarked baking sheet.

4 For the meringue layers, divide the remaining mixture between the prepared baking sheets and spread out evenly within the marked rectangles (see page 49).

5 Bake the meringue batons in the preheated oven for 45 minutes–1 hour and bake the rectangles for 1½–2 hours, until crisp and dry. Remove from the oven and let cool on wire racks. Lift off the baking parchment.

6 For the filling, whip the cream, sugar, and Tia Maria into soft peaks. Put one meringue rectangle on a serving plate and spread with a quarter of the cream. Repeat twice more, ending with a layer of cream.

7 Spoon the remaining whipped cream into a pastry bag fitted with a ½ in (1cm) star nozzle. Pipe in a shell design around the top edge of the Tranche (see page 145). Arrange the meringue batons down the center and dust with cocoa powder just before serving.

Oven temperature
250°F/120°C

Baking time
45 minutes–1 hour for the meringue batons, 1½–2 hours for the meringue rectangles

Cake pans
Four flat baking sheets, lined with baking parchment

Makes
10 slices

Storage
Best eaten as soon as it is made

Japonais

This classic French pastry is usually seen in the pâtissier's shop window. Instantly recognizable, each small, flat disk has a single toasted nut set in the middle of the finely chopped nut topping. It looks difficult to make but is really quite simple. While almonds and a mocha filling are traditional, this larger version is made with toasted hazelnuts (see page 45) and filled with chocolate ganache. (See page 20 for illustration.)

INGREDIENTS

For the Japonais

⅔ cup (150g) superfine sugar

1 cup (100g) toasted hazelnuts, finely ground (see page 45)

6 tbsp (45g) confectioners' sugar

4 tsp potato starch

4 egg whites

For the filling and decoration

1 quantity chocolate ganache (see page 151)

4 tbsp toasted hazelnuts, finely chopped

8 whole toasted hazelnuts

1 Mark two 9½ in (24cm) circles on the prepared baking sheets. Mix half the superfine sugar with the hazelnuts, confectioners' sugar, and potato starch.

2 Whisk the egg whites into soft peaks. Gradually whisk in the remaining superfine sugar to form a stiff, glossy meringue. Fold in the nut and sugar mixture and mix evenly.

3 Spead the mixture equally within the marked circles (see page 49) and bake in the preheated oven for 1 hour. Remove from the oven and let cool on a wire rack. Lift off the baking parchment.

4 Spread half the ganache over the base of one meringue disk. Cover with the second disk, smooth side up. Spread the remaining ganache over the top and sides of the cake.

5 Press most of the chopped nuts onto the sides (see page 143), arrange the whole nuts around the top, and sprinkle the center with the remaining nuts.

 Oven temperature
325°F/160°C

 Baking time
1 hour

 Cake pans
Two flat baking sheets, lined with baking parchment

 Makes
12 slices

 Storage
Keeps for 4–5 days

 Freezing
Freezes for 1–2 months

 Step ahead
Prepare the toasted hazelnuts; make the chocolate ganache

Lemon Meringue Pie

A fine combination of contrasting flavors is created in this sharp and tart lemon cream with a sweet, crisp pastry, topped with a soft cloud of meringue. It is not unlike the Elizabethan sweet-filled "royal pye," which was iced with sugar and egg white.

INGREDIENTS

For the pie shell

1 quantity pâte brisée pastry (see page 54)

For the filling

¼ cup (60g) cornstarch

⅔ cup (150g) granulated sugar

1 cup (250ml) water

finely grated zest of 1 lemon

½ cup (125ml) lemon juice

2 tbsp butter

4 egg yolks

For the topping

4 egg whites

¼ tsp cream of tartar

⅔ cup (150g) superfine sugar

1 Allow the pastry to come back to room temperature. Knead briefly on a lightly floured surface, roll out, and use to line the prepared tart pan (see page 56). Bake with pie weights for 10 minutes (see page 56). Uncover and bake for 4–5 minutes, until golden. Remove from the oven. Let cool. Lower the temperature.

2 For the filling, blend the cornstarch, sugar, water, and lemon zest and juice in a pan. Slowly bring to a boil, stirring constantly, until thickened and clear. Cook gently for 1 minute.

3 Stir in the butter. Beat 2 tablespoons of the hot lemon mixture into the egg yolks, then gradually beat the yolks into the lemon mixture. Return to the heat and cook gently, stirring, for 1 minute. Remove from the heat and spread into the pie shell.

4 For the topping, whisk the egg whites and cream of tartar into soft peaks. Gradually whisk in the sugar to form a stiff, glossy meringue (see page 49). Spread over the pie to make a seal with the pastry edge. Swirl with the tip of a knife and bake for 10 minutes, or until golden.

Oven temperature
425°F/220°C for the pie shell; 350°F/180°C for the topping

Baking time
14–15 minutes for the pie shell; 10 minutes for the topping

Tart pan
9in (23cm) fluted tart pan or nonstick pie plate, greased

Makes
6–8 slices

Storage
Best eaten the day it is made

Step ahead
Make the pastry and chill for 1 hour

Pastries & Cookies

Homemade pastries and cookies always add a welcoming note to any invitation for tea or coffee. Here are crisp-baked, toffeelike wafers full of nuts and glacé fruit, light and crunchy sugar cookies rich in butter, crisp cream puffs filled with fresh berries nestling in softly whipped cream, and wafer-thin almond cookies shaped like curved roof tiles. These delectable mouthfuls of sweet refreshment are always appreciated and hard to resist, so be sure to make plenty. If there are any left, store them in an airtight container.

A SELECTION OF
Butter Cookies,
Florentines, and
Bienenstich

Florentines

Florentines are a luxurious version of the old-fashioned brandy snap. Crisp and lacy, they can be coated with melted chocolate – semisweet, milk, or white. Mark the chocolate lightly with a fork if you want the cookies to look a little more fancy (see page 146). Bake no more than five cookies at a time and watch them carefully; they burn very easily.

INGREDIENTS

¾ cup (90g) sliced almonds

¼ cup (30g) unblanched almonds, coarsely chopped

¼ cup (45g) candied orange and lemon peel, finely chopped

½ cup (30g) glacé cherries, washed, dried, and cut into small pieces

1 tbsp angelica, washed, dried, and cut into small pieces (optional)

1 tbsp all-purpose flour

scant ½ cup (100g) butter

scant ½ cup (100g) granulated sugar

2 tbsp clear honey

2 tbsp heavy cream

7oz (200g) semisweet chocolate, melted (see page 44) to decorate

1 Mix together the sliced and chopped almonds, peel, glacé cherries, angelica, and flour.

2 Put the butter, sugar, honey, and cream in a pan. Heat gently to dissolve the sugar. Bring to a boil and cook to 250°F/120°C.

3 Stir in the fruit and nut mixture and cook, stirring, for 1 minute, until the mixture rolls off the sides of the pan. Remove from the heat.

4 Drop 5 rounded teaspoons of the mixture 3in (7cm) apart on the prepared baking sheet and flatten each to a circle about 2½in (6cm) in diameter with the back of the spoon. Bake in the preheated oven for 8–10 minutes, until the edges are golden.

5 Remove from the oven and let cool for 3 minutes. Transfer to a wire rack with a metal spatula. Spread the back of each cookie with some of the melted chocolate (see page 146) and refrigerate to set.

 Oven temperature
350°F/180°C

 Baking time
8–10 minutes

 Cake pan
Flat baking sheet, lined with waxed paper

Makes
35 cookies

Storage
Keep refrigerated in an airtight container for 1–2 weeks

Bienenstich

A particular family favorite, these delicious buttery fingers are covered with an almond toffee topping. The fresher they are, the better they taste.

INGREDIENTS

For the topping

7 tbsp (100g) butter

scant ½ cup (100g) granulated sugar

2 tbsp light brown sugar

2 tbsp milk

2 cups (250g) sliced almonds

For the base

½ cup (125g) unsalted butter

½ cup (125g) granulated sugar

1 egg

1 tsp finely grated lemon zest

1¼ cups (200g) all-purpose flour, sifted

1 tsp baking powder

1 For the topping, melt the butter in a medium-size pan. Stir in the granulated sugar, brown sugar, and the milk. Bring to a rapid boil, stirring all the time, then remove from the heat and stir in the sliced almonds, making sure that all the nuts are well coated with the toffee. Set aside and let cool slightly.

2 For the base, beat the butter and sugar together until pale and fluffy. Beat in the egg and lemon zest. Sift the flour and baking powder together. Gradually beat into the butter mixture until evenly mixed.

3 Spread the base mixture evenly into the prepared pan and lightly level the surface. Spoon on the almond topping and spread it out carefully.

4 Bake in the preheated oven for 35 minutes, or until golden. Remove from the oven and immediately cut into slices before the topping hardens. Let rest in the pan until cold. Remove from the pan and peel off the lining paper to serve.

 Oven temperature
350°F/180°C

 Baking time
35 minutes

 Cake pan
9in (23cm) shallow, square pan, greased and lined

 Makes
15 slices

 Storage
Keep for 4–5 days

Butter Cookies

These piped cookies are crisp on the outside and slightly soft in the center. Dip in melted chocolate once they are cool.

INGREDIENTS

½ cup (125g) butter

½ cup (125g) confectioners' sugar

2 small eggs, lightly beaten

1 tsp finely grated lemon zest

½ cup (60g) ground almonds

1⅔ cups (200g) all-purpose flour, sifted

7oz (200g) semisweet, milk, or white chocolate, melted (see page 44) to decorate

1 Beat the butter and sugar together until pale and fluffy. Beat in the eggs and lemon zest. Stir in alternating spoonfuls of the ground almonds and flour until evenly mixed. Cover and chill for 30 minutes.

2 Spoon some mixture into a large pastry bag fitted with a ½in (1cm) star nozzle. Pipe S-shapes, rings, or long sticks about 1in (2.5cm) apart on the prepared baking sheets. Chill for 30 minutes.

3 Bake in the preheated oven for 10 minutes, or until golden. Let cool on the baking sheets. Dip the cookies into the melted chocolate and let set on waxed paper.

 Oven temperature
375°F/190°C

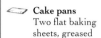 **Baking time**
10 minutes

 Cake pans
Two flat baking sheets, greased

 **Makes**
24 cookies

Storage
Keep for 4–5 days

❄ **Freezing**
Freeze for 1–2 months, undecorated

Sugar Cookies

When I was a child my mother used to make these favorite cookies regularly. My sister and I loved to help her cut out the shapes and then finish them with egg and sugar. (See page 25 for illustration.)

INGREDIENTS

2 cups (250g) all-purpose flour, sifted

1 cup (250g) chilled butter, diced

½ cup (125g) granulated sugar

1 tsp finely grated lemon zest

2 eggs, lightly beaten

granulated, light brown, and colored sugar crystals to decorate

1 Cut the flour and butter together into a fine crumblike mixture. Stir in the granulated sugar, lemon zest, and half the beaten egg. Knead briefly on a surface lightly dusted with flour until smooth. Cover with plastic wrap and chill for 30 minutes.

2 Roll out thinly on a lightly floured surface. Cut into shapes using 2in (5cm) cutters. Knead and reroll the trimmings, until you have about 60 cookies.

3 Space ½in (1cm) apart on the prepared baking sheets, brush with the remaining egg, and sprinkle the centers with sugar. Bake in the preheated oven for 10–12 minutes, until golden. Let cool on a wire rack.

 Oven temperature
375°F/190°C

Baking time
10–12 minutes

 Cake pans
Two or three flat baking sheets, greased

 **Makes**
60 cookies

 Storage
Keep for 2 weeks

Tuiles

A tuile is a wafer-thin cookie shaped like a traditional curved French roof tile. Once baked, the soft toffeelike pastry needs to be quickly shaped and then left until crisp, so do not try to make more than five at a time. (See page 25 for illustration.)

INGREDIENTS

½ cup (60g) ground almonds

½ cup (75g) sliced almonds plus 2 tbsp

¼ cup (60g) granulated sugar

1 tbsp all-purpose flour, sifted

1 egg white, lightly beaten

2 tbsp butter, melted and cooled

1 tsp dark rum

1 Put the ground almonds, ½ cup (75g) sliced almonds, sugar, and flour in a bowl. Stir in the egg white, butter, and rum. Chill, covered, for 3 hours.

2 Drop 5 rounded teaspoons of the mixture, 5in (12cm) apart, onto the prepared baking sheet. Flatten each to ⅛in (2.5mm) thick, sprinkle with the remaining sliced almonds, and bake in the preheated oven for 6–8 minutes, or until golden.

3 Remove from the oven, scoop up with a metal spatula, and press over a rolling pin. Let set for 2–3 minutes, then transfer to a wire rack and let cool. Repeat with the remaining mixture.

Oven temperature
325°F/160°C

Baking time
6–8 minutes

Cake pan
Flat baking sheet, greased

Makes
16 cookies

Storage
Keep for 1 week

Fruit & Cream Puffs

These light and airy cream puffs make a lovely afternoon treat or summertime dessert. The raw, piped pastry mixture can be made a few days ahead and frozen, then baked directly from the freezer for five minutes longer than normal.

INGREDIENTS

For the pastry

*1 quantity choux pastry
(see page 57)*

For the filling and decoration

1¼ cups (300ml) heavy cream

2 tbsp granulated sugar

*2 cups (250g) fresh fruit
such as raspberries, blueberries,
and sliced kiwi*

confectioners' sugar

1 Make the choux pastry (see page 57) and spoon into a pastry bag fitted with a ½in (1cm) star nozzle.

2 Pipe the mixture into twelve 3in (7.5cm) mounds on the prepared baking sheet. Carefully brush with the beaten egg left over from making the pastry. Bake in the preheated oven for 25 minutes, or until puffed up, crisp, and golden.

3 Remove from the oven and pierce a hole in the bottom of each puff with a fine metal skewer. Return to the oven, upside down, for 5 minutes to dry out. Remove from the oven and let cool on a wire rack.

4 Slice each puff horizontally in half. For the filling, whip the cream and sugar into soft peaks. Spoon into a pastry bag fitted with a ½in (1cm) star nozzle and pipe generously into the bottom of each puff.

5 Arrange a few berries or pieces of kiwi on top of the cream and then cover each puff with its top. Dust with a little confectioners' sugar to decorate.

 Oven temperature
425°F/220°C

 Baking time
30 minutes

 Cake pan
Flat baking sheet, lightly greased, run under cold water and left slightly wet

 Makes
12 puffs

 Storage
Best eaten as soon as they are made

Chocolate Éclairs

A mouthwatering combination of crisp pastry, rich crème pâtissière, and dark melted chocolate.

INGREDIENTS

For the pastry

*1 quantity choux pastry
(see page 57)*

For the filling and decoration

⅔ cup (90ml) heavy cream

*1 quantity crème pâtissière
(see page 151)*

4oz (125g) semisweet chocolate

1 Make the choux pastry (see page 57) and spoon into a pastry bag fitted with a ½in (1cm) plain nozzle. Pipe twelve 4in (10cm) lines of pastry 2in (5cm) apart onto the prepared baking sheet. Carefully brush with the beaten egg left over from making the pastry.

2 Bake in the preheated oven for 20 minutes, or until crisp and golden. Remove from the oven and pierce a small hole in the bottom of each one with a fine metal skewer. Return to the oven, upside down, for 3–5 minutes to dry out.

Remove from the oven and let cool on a wire rack.

3 Slice each éclair horizontally in half. For the filling, whip the cream into stiff peaks then fold into the crème pâtissière, until evenly mixed. Spoon into a pastry bag fitted with a ½in (1cm) star nozzle. Pipe into the bottom of each éclair and then cover with the top.

4 Melt the chocolate (see page 44). Let cool slightly, until thickened but not set. Carefully dip the top of each éclair into the melted chocolate or spread the top of each one with chocolate using a narrow spatula. Place chocolate side up on a wire rack to set.

VARIATION

Dip the tops of the éclairs in 1 quantity of vanilla, coffee, or chocolate glacé icing (see page 152) instead of the melted chocolate. Let set.

 Oven temperature
425°F/220°C

 Baking time
23–25 minutes

 Cake pan
Flat baking sheet, lightly greased, run under cold water and left slightly wet

 Makes
12 éclairs

 Storage
Best eaten as soon as they are made

 Step ahead
Make the crème pâtissière

Wedding Cakes

Many of the customs surrounding a wedding ceremony, the feast, and the cake are symbols of sharing between the bride and groom and their guests. In Roman times the cake was simply made of flour, water or wine, and honey, but by the 18th century it had become a multi-layered extravaganza, with great importance being given to the elaborate decoration made of sugar paste, marzipan, and spun sugar depicting architectural and sculptural themes.

Croquembouche

This French confection is made of ingredients that crunch and crumble in the mouth, hence the name "croque-em-bouche." In earlier times, small cakes, fruit, or pieces of spun sugar were stuck together with sugar syrup inside a plain, molded container. When the containers were briefly heated and turned over, the cake would drop out. The familiar choux pastry pyramid is a recent innovation and is the most popular celebration cake in France today.

INGREDIENTS

For the paper cone

one 25x20in (62.5x50cm) sheet of posterboard

For the pastry base

1½ quantities pâte brisée pastry (see page 54)

For the cream puffs

4 quantities choux pastry (see page 57)

For the filling

10 cups (2.5 liters) heavy cream

½–¼ cup (125–180g) granulated sugar

½–¼ cup (125–170ml) brandy

For the caramel glaze

4½ cups (1kg) granulated sugar

1⅓ cups (300ml) water

small pinch of cream of tartar

For the decoration

selection of fresh white and lilac flowers

TO MAKE THE CONE

1 Lay the posterboard flat, long side facing you. Make a mark halfway along the top long edge. Draw diagonal lines from this point down to the two bottom corners. Fold along these lines to create a large triangle.

2 Fold this triangle in half, leaving all the excess posterboard inside for strength. Measure 20in (50cm) from the narrowest point down each long side and make a mark. Draw a gentle curve from one mark to the other. Cut carefully along the line. This gives a level base to help the cone stand upright.

3 Bend the posterboard into a cone so that the two long edges meet. Stick together with plenty of adhesive tape. Push some foil or tissue paper inside the cone for extra stability. The finished cone should measure 20in (50cm) in height with the base 8in (20cm) in diameter.

TO MAKE THE CAKE

1 For the base, allow the pastry to come back to room temperature. Knead briefly until smooth and roll out on a lightly floured surface into a 12in (30cm) circle.

2 Transfer the pastry to the greased baking sheet and crimp the edge between your fingers. Prick all over with a fork and bake in the preheated oven for 15–20 minutes. Remove from the oven and let cool. Lower the oven temperature.

3 For the cream puffs, make the choux pastry (see page 57), one batch at a time. Spoon the first batch into a pastry bag fitted with a ½in (1cm) plain nozzle. Pipe the mixture onto the wet baking sheets, in small ½in (1cm) mounds.

4 Bake in the preheated oven for about 15 minutes, or until crisp and golden. Pierce a hole in the bottom of each puff with a fine metal skewer. Return to the oven, upside down, for 2–3 minutes to dry out. Remove

Oven temperature
400°F/200°C
for the pastry base;
425°F/220°C
for the puffs

Baking time
15–20 minutes for the pastry base;
15–20 minutes for the puffs

Cake pans
Three flat baking sheets, one lightly greased and the others run under cold water and left slightly wet

Makes
50–60 portions

Storage
Keeps for 2 hours once assembled

Freezing
Freeze the piped choux mixture for up to 1 month

Step ahead
Make and pipe the choux paste, freeze raw and bake from frozen for 20–25 minutes; make the pastry and chill for 1 hour; make the cone

from the oven and let cool on wire racks.

5 Repeat this process with the next three batches of pastry, very gradually enlarging the mounds of paste until they are about 1in (2.5cm) in size. As each batch of pastry is used, bake immediately (or freeze), increasing the baking time a little as the puffs get larger. The largest puffs will take about 20 minutes to cook. You will need about 150 puffs in total.

6 For the filling, whip the cream, sugar, and brandy into stiff peaks. Spoon a little at a time into a pastry bag fitted with a ¼in (5mm) plain nozzle. Pipe into each puff until each feels full, and chill for 1 hour.

TO ASSEMBLE THE CAKE

1 Put the pastry base on a large serving plate or cake board and place the cardboard cone in the center.

2 For the glaze, make the caramel in four batches as needed. For each batch, put 1¼ cups (250g) sugar and 6 tablespoons (75ml) water into a heavy-bottomed pan. Leave over low heat until the sugar has completely dissolved. Stir in the cream of tartar, increase the heat, and bring to a boil without stirring. Boil for about 7 minutes, or until the syrup reaches 345°F (173°C) and has turned a rich caramel color (see page 153).

3 Remove the pan from the heat and plunge the bottom into cold water. Let stand in a bowl of very hot water, to prevent the caramel from setting, while you assemble the cake.

4 Starting with the largest puffs, spear them one at a time on a skewer or fork. Dip the tops quickly into the caramel, covering them well. Slide off the skewer and position them side by side around the bottom of the cone. Make sure each one sticks well to the next.

5 Quickly position a second row of caramel-dipped puffs on top of the first, before they have time to set. Continue working like this, using the puffs in order of size, and making more caramel as you need it, until the cone is covered. Let set.

6 Cut the flower stems down to about ½in (1cm). Starting at the top, tuck them in between the puffs in a sweep. Keep in a cool, dry place. Serve within 2 hours.

Arrange the flowers in a decorative cascade

Stick the cream puffs together with caramel

Autumn Wedding Cake

The forerunner of this wedding cake was a two-tiered version that originated in 17th-century France. Unlike the plainer cakes of earlier times, this one was made with rich ingredients. One tier, the "groom's cake," was dark and heavily fruited. The lighter "bride's cake" was bedecked with spun sugar ornaments. Now, the cakes are more often carrot and butter cakes, sponges, and even cheesecakes. For this wedding cake, make two of each of the almond cake layers and then sandwich them together in pairs with buttercream before stacking them one on top of the other and decorating. (See page 26 for illustration.)

INGREDIENTS

For each 12in (30cm) orange and almond cake (bottom tier). Make two.

- 1½ cups (375g) unsalted butter, softened
- 1⅔ cups (375g) granulated sugar
- 6 eggs
- 2½ cups (375g) self-rising flour
- finely grated zest of 1 large orange
- 1 tsp almond extract
- 1 cup (125g) ground almonds
- ⅓ cup (75ml) fresh orange juice

For each 8in (20cm) chocolate and almond cake (middle tier). Make two.

- ¾ cup (180g) unsalted butter, softened
- ¾ cup (180g) granulated sugar
- 3 eggs, separated
- 6oz (180g) semisweet chocolate
- 2 tsp finely grated orange zest
- 1¼ cups (180g) self-rising flour, sifted
- ½ cup (60g) ground almonds
- 1 tbsp fresh orange juice

For each 6in (15cm) chocolate and almond cake (top tier). Make two.

- ½ cup (125g) unsalted butter, softened
- ½ cup (125g) granulated sugar
- 2 eggs, separated
- 4oz (125g) semisweet chocolate
- 1 tsp finely grated orange zest
- ¾ cup (100g) self-rising flour, sifted
- ⅓ cup (45g) ground almonds
- 2 tsp fresh orange juice

For the buttercream

- 3lb (1.5kg) unsalted butter, softened
- 5lb (2.5kg) confectioners' sugar, sifted
- ⅔ cup (150ml) fresh orange juice
- orange food coloring powder or liquid

To assemble the cake

- one 6in (15cm) thin cake board
- one 8in (20cm) thin cake board
- one 14in (35cm) thick cake board
- 1 small nylon pastry bag
- one ¹⁄₁₆ in (1.25mm) writing nozzle
- one ½ in (1cm) ribbon nozzle
- 12 acrylic or wooden cake dowels
- fresh orange-colored flowers
- 4in (10cm) sphere of florist's oasis
- 2¼ yards (2 meters) wide dark orange ribbon
- 2¼ yards (2 meters) narrow pale orange ribbon

1 For the 12in (30cm) orange and almond cake, beat the butter and sugar together until pale and fluffy. Beat in the eggs, one at a time, adding a little of the flour if the mixture begins to curdle. Stir in the orange zest and almond extract. Mix in the flour, almonds, and orange juice.

2 Spread the mixture into the prepared pan and bake in the preheated oven for 30–35 minutes, or until a skewer comes out clean. Remove from the oven and let cool in the pan. Turn out, peel off the lining paper, and wrap in foil if not using right away. Repeat for the second layer.

3 For the 8in (20cm) chocolate and almond cake, beat the butter, sugar, and egg yolks together until pale and fluffy. Melt the chocolate (see page 44), cool slightly, and then stir in with the orange zest. Stir in the flour, almonds, and orange juice.

4 In another bowl, whisk the egg whites into soft peaks. Fold 3 spoonfuls into the main mixture to loosen the texture, then gently fold in the rest. Pour into the prepared pan and bake for 25–30 minutes, or until a skewer comes out clean. Remove from the oven and let cool in the pan. Turn out, peel off the lining paper, and wrap in foil. Repeat for the second layer.

5 For the 6in (15cm) chocolate and almond cake, follow the method for the 8in (20cm) cake. Pour into the prepared pan and bake for 20–25 minutes, or until a skewer comes out clean. Repeat for the second layer.

Oven temperature
350°F/180°C

Baking time
30–35 minutes for each 12in (30cm) cake layer; 25–30 minutes for each 8in (20cm) cake layer; 20–25 minutes for each 6in (15cm) cake layer

Cake pans
One 12in (30cm), one 8in (20cm), and one 6in (15cm) deep, square pan, greased and lined

Makes
12in (30cm) cake makes 60 slices; 8in (20cm) cake makes 24 slices; 6in (15cm) cake makes 12 slices

Storage
The assembled cake keeps for up to 3 days, without the flower decoration

Freezing
The sponge cakes can be frozen for 1 month, undecorated

Step ahead
Make the buttercream and sponge layers up to 4 days in advance

6 For the buttercream, beat 1½ cups (375g) butter with 5 cups (625g) confectioners' sugar until smooth. Beat in up to 2½ tablespoons of the orange juice to give a spreading consistency. Repeat three times. Color one of the four batches orange using a little of the coloring powder.

7 Sandwich together the cakes in pairs with a little of the plain buttercream. Place each one on the appropriate board. Using a warm, dry narrow spatula, spread the top and sides of each cake with a thin layer of the plain buttercream.

8 Spoon the orange-colored buttercream into a pastry bag fitted with the writing nozzle (see page 145). Pipe an even number of vertical lines, about ½in (1cm) apart, over the sides of each cake and across the top of the smallest cake. Spoon the plain buttercream, a little at a time, into a pastry bag fitted with the ribbon nozzle.

9 Starting at the bottom of each cake, pipe horizontally over each alternate line to give a basketweave design (see page 145). For the next row up, start with the second vertical line in. On the third row, repeat the first line. Continue like this over all the cakes.

TO ASSEMBLE THE CAKE

1 Measure the depth of the bottom tier. Cut 8 dowels 1in (2.5cm) longer than this. Push them into the cake, in a square 3in (7.5cm) from the edge. Repeat for the middle tier with the remaining dowels, but insert them 2in (5cm) from the edge.

2 Carefully place the middle tier centrally over the bottom one, so that it rests on the dowels. Position the top tier in the same way. Trim the stalks of the flowers to about 1½in (3.5cm) long, and pack them between the tiers. Place the smaller flowers around the base of the bottom tier.

3 Slice off the top third of the oasis sphere and press in more flowers to cover it closely. Set on top of the cake. Trim the sides of the bottom cake board with the ribbons.

Traditional Wedding Cake

The dark, heavily-fruited "groom's cake" still remains the classic English celebration cake, while the decorative white icing on the outside represents the paler "bride's cake" of old. This wedding cake retains the early custom of light and dark layers; the top tier is a dark Traditional Plum Cake, a layer to be kept until later, for the first anniversary. The two lighter tiers are made of Baumkuchen, the classic German celebration cake. With its roots in pre-Christian Greece, this "tree" cake was once made by pouring the batter onto a wooden skewer turned by hand on a spit over an open fire. Today, thin layers of the batter are toasted one on top of the other in a pan, so they still resemble the rings of a tree when cut across. It should be served in very thin slices. (See page 27 for illustration.)

INGREDIENTS

For the 6in (15cm) Traditional Plum Cake (top tier)

- *½ cup (60g) dried cranberries*
- *⅓ cup (60g) dark raisins*
- *½ cup (90g) golden raisins*
- *½ cup (90g) currants*
- *½ cup (90g) dried apricots, chopped*
- *scant ⅓ cup (90ml) dark rum or brandy*
- *1½ tsp finely grated orange zest*
- *1 tbsp orange juice*
- *1 cup (150g) all-purpose flour*
- *1 tsp ground cinnamon*
- *¼ tsp ground allspice*
- *½ cup (60g) ground almonds*
- *½ cup (125g) butter*
- *⅔ cup (125g) light brown sugar*
- *2 large eggs, lightly beaten*

For the 9in (23cm) Baumkuchen (middle tier)

- *2 cups (500g) unsalted butter, softened*
- *seeds from ½ of a vanilla bean*
- *finely grated zest of 1 lemon*
- *2¼ cups (500g) granulated sugar*
- *14 eggs, separated*
- *1¾ cups (250g) all-purpose flour*
- *1¾ cups (250g) potato starch*

For the 12in (30cm) Baumkuchen (bottom tier)

- *4 cups (1kg) unsalted butter, softened*
- *seeds from 1 vanilla bean*
- *finely grated zest of 2 lemons*
- *4½ cups (1kg) granulated sugar*
- *28 eggs, separated*
- *3½ cups (500g) all-purpose flour*
- *3½ cups (500g) potato starch*

For the decoration

- *2 quantities apricot glaze (see page 149)*
- *6½ quantites marzipan (see page 152) or 6½lb (3.25kg) white marzipan*
- *8lb (4kg) champagne-colored sugar paste*
- *large assortment of cream and peach colored flowers such as spray roses*
- *4 egg whites*
- *2¼ cups (500g) superfine sugar*

To assemble the cake

- *one 8in (20cm) thick cake board*
- *one 16in (40cm) thick cake board*
- *one 10in (25cm) thin cake board*
- *5½ yards (5 meters) cream satin ribbon*
- *8 acrylic cake dowels*
- *3 hollow champagne-colored cake pillars*

1 Make the 6in (15cm) Plum Cake (see page 99 for the method). Spoon the mixture into the prepared pan and bake in the preheated oven for 2 hours, covering with waxed paper after 1 hour, or until a skewer comes out clean. Remove from the oven and let cool. Turn out, peel off the paper, and wrap in foil.

2 For the 9in (23cm) Baumkuchen, make the cake in two layers, using one 7-egg mixture for each layer. Beat 1 cup (250g) butter, half the vanilla, half the lemon zest, and 1⅛ cups (250g) sugar together until pale and fluffy. Beat in 7 egg yolks, one at a time. Sift together half each of the all-purpose flour and the potato starch. Gradually beat in until well combined. In another bowl, whisk the egg whites into soft peaks. Stir in 2 large spoonfuls, then carefully fold in the rest.

3 Preheat the broiler to high. Spread 6 tablespoons of the mixture evenly over the base of the smaller prepared pan. Broil for 2–3 minutes until golden and cooked through. Remove, cover with another layer of mixture, and broil for 2–3 minutes. After 3–4 layers, you will be able to spread the mixture more thinly. Continue, using 4 tablespoons of mixture for each layer. Remove the cake from the pan and let cool on a wire rack. Repeat to make the second layer.

4 For the two 12in (30cm) Baumkuchen layers, make up the mixture, one 7-egg batch at a time (see step 2). Spread

Oven temperature
300°F/150°C for the 6in (15cm) fruit cake

Baking time
2 hours for the 6in (15cm) fruit cake; about 1 hour broiling time for each 9in (23cm) Baumkuchen layer; about 2 hours broiling time for each 12in (30cm) Baumkuchen layer

Cake pans
One 6in (15cm) deep, round pan for the fruit cake, greased and lined; one 9in (23cm) springform pan and one 12in (30cm) springform pan, bases greased with butter and floured for the Baumkuchen

Makes
6in (15cm) cake makes 20 slices; 9in (23cm) cake makes 40 slices; 12in (30cm) cake makes 70 slices

Storage
6in (15cm) fruit cake will keep for several months in an airtight container; the Baumkuchen will keep fresh for 3–4 weeks, covered with plastic wrap and foil; the assembled cake will keep for up to 1 week without the flower decoration

Freezing
The fruit cake will freeze for 1 year

about 10 tablespoons of mixture over the base of the larger prepared pan and broil for 2–3 minutes. After 3–4 layers, reduce to 6–7 tablespoons of mixture. Continue as for the smaller cake, using two 7-egg batches for each layer.

5 Sandwich the two 9in (23cm) Baumkuchen layers together with 2 tablespoons of apricot glaze and the 12in (30cm) layers together with 3–4 tablespoons of glaze. Brush the 6in (15cm) fruit cake with 1–2 tablespoons of glaze. Cover with ¾lb (375g) marzipan (see page 140). Brush the 9in (23cm) Baumkuchen with 3–4 tablespoons of glaze and cover with 2lb (1kg) marzipan. Brush the 12in (30cm) Baumkuchen with 5–6 tablespoons of glaze and cover with 3½lb (1.75kg) marzipan.

6 Cover the 8in (20cm) thick cake board with ½lb (250g) sugar paste and the 16in (40cm) thick board with 1lb (500g) sugar paste (see page 141). Let dry for at least 24 hours. Moisten the marzipan surface of each cake (see page 140). Cover the fruit cake in 1lb (500g) sugar paste, the 9in (23cm) Baumkuchen in 2lb (1kg) sugar

paste, and the 12in (30cm) Baumkuchen in 3½lb (1.75kg) sugar paste (see page 141). Place the 9in (23cm) cake on the thin board and trim the thick boards with some ribbon.

TO ASSEMBLE THE CAKE

1 Place the 6in (15cm) and the 12in (30cm) cakes on the thick boards. Measure the depth of the 12in (30cm) cake and cut 5 dowels to the same length. Push into the cake, in an evenly spaced circle, about 3in (7cm) from the edge. Measure the depth of the 9in (23cm) cake and the height of the cake pillars and cut the remaining dowels to the length of their combined measurements.

2 Push the dowels into the 9in (23cm) cake in an evenly spaced circle, about 3in (7cm) in from the edge. Position the cake centrally on top of the 12in (30cm) cake. Slide the cake pillars over the dowels and rest the smallest cake on top. Attach ribbon around the base of each cake. Sugar-frost the flowers using the egg white and superfine sugar (see page 148) and let dry. Arrange over the cake no more than 6 hours before serving.

Festival Cakes

Preparing a cake for a special occasion, whether religious or secular, has long been a ritual. As a result, many rich and luxurious recipes have passed from generation to generation. Indeed, the tradition of baking has its origins in the feasts and festivals of the distant past – spices, dried fruit, and nuts, which were once coveted and costly ingredients, were reserved especially for such times.

THE CAKE'S TEXTURE *is dense and honey-enriched, studded with nuts and dried fruit, and lightly marbled with chocolate.*

Certosino

Special Ingredients

Golden raisins *can be plumped up in hot water for 30 minutes before using.*

Dark rum *imparts rich, sweet moisture.*

Honey *with a fine aroma and clear tones makes the best sweetener.*

Cinnamon *adds an intense aromatic taste.*

Aniseed *gives the cake its distinctive licorice flavor.*

Apple purée *adds a moist, rich texture.*

Candied fruit, walnuts, and pecans *are traditional festive decorations.*

Almonds *are blanched in boiling water, then sliced into thin flakes.*

Semisweet chocolate *must be high in cocoa fat for a good flavor.*

Pine nuts *have a mild but delicious resinous flavor.*

Making the Cake

This is a traditional Italian Christmas cake that originated with the Carthusian monks of Bologna during medieval times. It is decorated with a sumptuous assortment of nuts and candied fruit.

INGREDIENTS

For the cake

½ cup (75g) golden raisins
1½ tbsp dark rum
1½ cups (350g) honey
3 tbsp butter
3 tbsp water
2 tsp aniseed
scant 3¼ cups (400g) all-purpose flour
1½ tsp baking soda
1 tsp ground cinnamon
¼ cup (400g) apple purée (see page 149)
1½ cups (180g) blanched almonds, coarsely chopped or sliced
2½ oz (75g) semisweet chocolate, coarsely chopped
¼ cup (180g) candied orange and lemon peel, finely chopped
3 tbsp pine nuts

For the decoration

3 tbsp apricot glaze (see page 149)
1½–2lb (750g–1kg) candied fruit, candied peel, walnut or pecan halves

1 For the cake, put the golden raisins and rum in a small bowl. Cover with plastic wrap and let soak for 30 minutes.

2 Put the honey, butter, and water together in a heavy-bottomed pan. Set over low heat and leave until melted. Stir in the aniseed.

3 Sift the flour, baking soda, and cinnamon into a large bowl. Slowly pour in the honey mixture and mix thoroughly until smooth. Stir in the apple purée, almonds, chocolate, candied peel, rum-soaked golden raisins, and pine nuts.

4 Spoon the mixture into the prepared pan and bake in the preheated oven for 1 hour–1 hour 10 minutes. Remove from the oven and invert onto a wire rack. Peel off the lining paper and let cool.

5 To decorate, brush the top of the cake with half the apricot glaze. Arrange the candied fruit, candied peel, and nuts decoratively over the cake and then brush once more with the remaining glaze. Let set before serving or storing.

 Oven temperature
325°F/160°C

 Baking time
1 hour–1 hour 10 minutes

 Cake pan
9in (23cm) springform pan, greased and lined

 Makes
16 slices

 Storage
Keeps for 1 week

 Step ahead
Make the apple purée; soak the golden raisins

Pumpkin Pie for Thanksgiving

Pumpkins ripen in October, just in time for Halloween. This pie makes a fitting end to a Thanksgiving feast, and the gingery snap adds an extra dimension of surprise. Serve with whipped cream on the side.

INGREDIENTS

For the pie shell

1 quantity pâte sucrée pastry (see page 55)

For the filling

2 cups (500ml) pumpkin purée (see page 149)
scant ½ cup (100g) granulated sugar
4 eggs
¾ cup (175ml) heavy cream
1 tsp ground cinnamon
pinch of ground cloves
pinch of ground mace
2 tbsp sherry, dark rum, or Cognac
¼ cup (60g) preserved ginger, drained and finely chopped (optional)

1 Allow the pastry to come back to room temperature.

Knead briefly until smooth, roll out on a floured surface, and use to line the prepared pan (see page 56). Prick all over with a fork and bake with pie weights (see page 56) in the preheated oven for 20 minutes. Remove from the oven, uncover, and let cool. Lower the oven temperature.

2 For the filling, beat the pumpkin purée, sugar, and eggs together. Stir in the heavy cream, spices, sherry, or rum or Cognac, and preserved ginger.

3 Pour the mixture into the pie shell and bake in the oven for 40 minutes, or until the filling is set. Remove from the pan and cool slightly before serving.

Oven temperature
400°F/200°C for the pie shell;
375°F/190°C for the filling

Baking time
20 minutes for the pie shell;
40 minutes for the filling

Tart pan
8½ in (22cm) fluted tart pan, greased

Makes
8 slices

Storage
Keeps for 1–2 days

Step ahead
Make the pastry

Bûche de Noël

It is difficult to trace the earliest date of this very popular, traditional French Christmas cake, but an early 20th-century pastry book gives a long and complicated description using a Genoise sponge roulade as a base. The log is decorated to look like a fallen tree covered with lichen and wood shavings, and sprouting small fungi.

INGREDIENTS

For the cake

1 quantity Biscuit de Savoie sponge mixture (see page 65)

For the filling

2 cups (450ml) heavy cream
¼ cup (60g) granulated sugar
1 tbsp Grand Marnier (optional)
1 tbsp finely grated orange zest

For the decoration

1½ quantities chocolate ganache (see page 151)
1–2 tbsp chopped blanched pistachio nuts
1–2 tbsp toasted sliced almonds
1 quantity meringue mushrooms (see page 148)
cocoa powder and confectioners' sugar

1 Make the Biscuit de Savoie sponge mixture (see page 65). Pour into the prepared pans and bake in the preheated oven for 10 minutes, swapping the trays from one shelf to the other after 5 minutes.

2 Remove from the oven, cover with waxed paper and slightly damp dish towels, and let cool. For the filling, whip

the cream, granulated sugar, Grand Marnier, and orange zest together into stiff peaks.

3 Uncover the sponges and invert onto waxed paper sprinkled with granulated sugar. Peel off the lining paper, trim the edges, and spread over the cream. Starting with one short edge, roll up (see page 53). Cut a thin slice off each end of one roll. Cut the second roll in half.

TO FINISH THE CAKE

1 Lay the whole cake and one half end to end and seam side down, on a serving plate. Diagonally cut one third off the remaining piece of cake. Position the larger piece at an angle on one side of the log, and the smaller piece, cut side up, on top. Spread the ganache over the top and sides of the log. Chill for 1 hour.

2 Decorate the chocolate log with the chopped pistachio nuts and meringue mushrooms. Dust with a little cocoa powder and confectioners' sugar.

Oven temperature
450°F/230°C

Baking time
10 minutes

Cake pans
Two 9½ x 13½ x ½ in (24x34x1cm) jelly roll pans, greased and lined

Makes
20–24 slices

Storage
Keeps for 3–4 days

Freezing
Freezes for 1 month, undecorated

Step ahead
Make the meringue mushrooms

Paskha

Unlike the traditional festive yeasted fruit breads of Russia, Paskha is a fruited and spiced cheesecake. It was traditionally pressed into a wooden pyramid-shaped mold carved with an Orthodox cross. (See page 17 for illustration.)

INGREDIENTS

1 cup (250g) unsalted butter, softened
¾ cup (180g) granulated sugar
1lb (500g) farmer cheese
2 egg yolks
½ cup (125ml) heavy cream
3 drops of vanilla extract
½ cup (125g) raisins
⅓ cup (60g) candied orange and lemon peel, finely chopped
2 tbsp chopped blanched pistachio nuts
1 cup (125g) toasted blanched almonds, chopped
1 cup (250g) candied clementines, citron, and other candied fruit to decorate

1 Beat the butter and sugar together until pale and fluffy. Beat in the farmer cheese until smooth, followed by the egg yolks, one at a time. Stir in the heavy cream and vanilla extract. Add the raisins, candied peel, chopped pistachio nuts, and almonds. Stir gently until everything is evenly mixed.

2 Spoon the mixture into the prepared mold and press down lightly. Lift the excess cloth over the top of the filling and tuck in around the edge. Lay a small plate inside the rim so that it sits on the mixture and place a heavy weight on top. Set the mold on a plate and chill for 6 hours or overnight.

3 Shortly before serving, invert the Paskha onto a plate. Carefully lift off the pot, then the cheesecloth. Thinly slice the candied clementines and citron and arrange around the base of the Paskha. Cut the remaining fruit into small diamonds and arrange in four crosses on opposite sides of the Paskha, together with a smaller one on top. Serve in thin slices.

 Cake mold
Flowerpot, 6in (15cm) across the top and 5½in (14cm) high, lined with several layers of damp cheesecloth

 Makes
10–12 slices

 Storage
Keeps for 2–3 days

Warning
This recipe contains raw eggs (see page 9)

Swiss Carnival Wafers

These crisp, disk-shaped delicacies are deep-fried in oil and then heavily dusted with confectioners' sugar. Use an oil with an indistinct flavor for cooking, such as corn, sunflower, or canola oil.

INGREDIENTS

2 eggs
2 tbsp granulated sugar
¼ cup (60ml) heavy cream
1¼ cups (250g) all-purpose flour, sifted
pinch of salt
finely grated zest of 1 lemon
2 tbsp vanilla sugar
oil for deep-frying
3 tbsp confectioners' sugar to decorate

1 Beat the eggs and sugar together well until thick, pale, and creamy. Gradually beat in the cream.

2 Sift together the flour and the salt. Gently fold half into the egg mixture with the lemon zest and vanilla sugar.

3 Add the remaining flour and mix into a soft dough. If the mixture is still sticky, mix in a little extra flour. Knead briefly on a floured surface, until smooth. Cover with plastic wrap and chill for 1–2 hours.

4 Divide the mixture equally into 20 pieces. Shape each piece into a ball and then roll out on a lightly floured work surface into wafer-thin disks about 5in (12cm) in diameter. Brush off any excess flour.

5 Heat the oil in a large, deep pan to 360°F (180°C), or until a cube of bread browns and rises to the top in 1 minute.

6 Drop the disks one at a time into the hot oil and cook for 12–15 seconds, or until puffed up, crisp, and golden. Turn and fry for another 5 seconds. Lift out with a slotted spoon and let drain on a wire rack covered with paper towels. Dust heavily with the confectioners' sugar when cold.

 Makes
20 wafers

 Storage
Keep for at least 2 weeks

Swedish Saffron Braid for Sankta Lucia

In celebration of Sankta Lucia, the Swedish festival of light that falls on December 13th, the youngest girl in a family wears a long white gown and a crown of lingonberry leaves ringed with candles. She awakens her parents very early in the morning and offers them a tray set with coffee and freshly baked saffron buns. This is a similar dough, shaped into a braided loaf.

INGREDIENTS

1 cup (250ml) milk
6 tbsp (90g) butter
½ tsp saffron
3½ cups (500g) all-purpose flour
2 envelopes rapid-rise dry yeast
½ cup (125g) granulated sugar
pinch of salt
1 egg yolk
½ cup (90g) raisins
½ cup (90g) chopped mixed peel
½ cup (60g) blanched almonds, finely chopped

For the decoration

1 egg, lightly beaten
1 tbsp chopped blanched almonds
1 tbsp crystal sugar

1 Heat the milk and butter in a small pan until the butter has melted. Stir in the saffron and let cool slightly.

2 Sift the flour, yeast, sugar, and salt together into a large bowl. Make a well in the center and add the buttery milk and the egg yolk. Gradually mix the flour into the liquid ingredients, adding a little more flour if the mixture is too wet, until it forms a ball of soft dough.

3 Knead the dough on a lightly floured surface for 10 minutes, until smooth and elastic. Place in a large bowl, cover with plastic wrap, and let rest in a warm place for 1½ hours, or until doubled in size.

4 Turn out the dough and knead for 5 minutes more. Knead in the raisins, mixed peel, and almonds. Cut into three even-sized pieces.

TO SHAPE THE BRAID

1 Knead each piece of dough into a ball and then roll each one into a 14in (35cm) long rope. Lightly braid the three pieces together and tuck the loose ends underneath.

2 Transfer the braid to the prepared baking sheet, cover with a dry cloth, and let rest in a warm place for 45 minutes, or until doubled in size.

3 Uncover the braid and brush with the egg. Sprinkle with the almonds and sugar and bake in the preheated oven for 30–40 minutes. Cover with foil if it starts to overbrown. Let cool on a wire rack.

Oven temperature
350°F/180°C

Baking time
30–40 minutes

Cake pan
Flat baking sheet, greased

Makes
18 slices

Storage
Keeps for 1 week

Freezing
Freezes for 2 months

Italian Easter Cake

Here is an unusual Easter cake from Naples that uses two traditional Italian ingredients: ricotta cheese and vermicelli pasta, which are baked in a sweet "pasta frolla" shortcrust pastry case.

INGREDIENTS

For the pasta frolla pastry

1⅔ cups (180g) all-purpose flour

pinch of salt

½ cup (125g) butter, cut into pieces

½ cup (100g) granulated sugar

3 egg yolks, lightly beaten

1 tsp finely grated lemon zest

For the filling

1½ cups (350ml) milk

½ cup (60g) small broken pieces of vermicelli or angel hair pasta

pinch of salt

½–¾ tsp ground cinnamon

⅔ cup (150g) granulated sugar

1½ cups (375g) ricotta cheese

3 eggs, separated

⅓ cup (60g) candied orange and lemon peel, finely chopped

1½ tbsp lemon juice

½ tsp finely grated lemon zest

3 tbsp dark rum

confectioners' sugar to decorate

1 For the pastry, sift the flour and salt into a bowl. Make a well in the center, add the butter, sugar, egg yolks, and lemon zest, and gradually mix together with a butter knife until everything starts to stick together. Knead gently on a lightly floured surface until smooth. Cover with plastic wrap and chill for 30 minutes.

2 For the filling, bring the milk to a boil. Add the vermicelli, salt, a pinch of the cinnamon, and 1 tablespoon of sugar. Simmer, uncovered, for 15–20 minutes, stirring now and then, until all the liquid has been absorbed. Let cool.

3 Beat together the cheese and scant ½ cup (100g) sugar until smooth. Beat in the egg yolks and vermicelli, followed by the remaining cinnamon, candied peels, lemon juice, zest, and rum.

4 In another bowl, whisk 2 egg whites into soft peaks. Whisk in the remaining sugar. Gently fold into the cheese mixture.

5 Set aside one third of the pastry. Press the remainder into the bottom and sides of the pan to within 1½in (3cm) of the top. Prick well with a fork and pour in the filling. Use the rest of the pastry for the lattice top (see below). Seal the strips onto the pastry edge, then trim.

6 Brush the pastry with the remaining egg white. Place in the preheated oven, lower the temperature, and bake for 1 hour, or until set and golden. Remove and let cool on a wire rack. Take out of the pan and dust with confectioners' sugar to decorate.

Oven temperature
400°F/200°C,
then
350°F/180°C

Baking time
1 hour

Cake pan
9in (23cm) springform pan, lightly greased

Makes
10 slices

Storage
Best eaten the day it is made

Making a Pastry Lattice

1 *Roll out the pastry on a lightly floured surface and cut into twelve ½in (1cm) wide strips using a pastry wheel or a knife.*

2 *Lay six of the strips, side by side, about 1in (2.5cm) apart, over the top of the cake, letting the edges overhang.*

3 *Lay the remaining strips across at right angles to the first, weaving them under and over to make a lattice pattern.*

Lightly dust the top of the cake with sugar before serving.

Children's Party Cakes

"And they saw that the little house was built of bread, and covered with little cakes; but the windows were made of pale sugar." In the 19th century, German bakers, inspired by this fairy-tale house from *Hansel and Gretel*, created a cake made of spiced dough, covered with white icing, bonbons, and chocolate. The magic remains today in children's birthday cakes that are brightly colored and decorated with candy and chocolates.

Little Houses

A Christmas fair is held each year in Nürnberg, Germany, where festive trinkets, cakes, spicy cookies, and little gingerbread houses are sold. My recipe uses simple sponge cakes cut into small house shapes, covered with sugar paste and decorated with icing or even favorite sweets. For large numbers of children, you can set several cakes in a row to create a street of houses.

INGREDIENTS

For the cake

½ quantity Victorian Sandwich Cake mixture (see page 66)

For the decoration

4 tbsp apricot glaze (see page 149)

8oz (250g) sugar paste (see page 152)

food coloring paste

2 cups (250g) confectioners' sugar, sifted

1 egg white

chocolate sticks, square chocolate thins, or chocolate buttons for the roofs

1 Make the Victoria Sandwich Cake mixture and spoon into the prepared pan. Bake in the preheated oven for 1 hour, or until a skewer comes out clean. Invert onto a wire rack and let cool. Peel off the lining paper.

2 Cut the cake crosswise into two shorter blocks and separate. Slice off the two corners from each cut end to make the roofs. Trim the other sides flat to give two 3in (7cm) cubes with a roof shape on top. Brush with the apricot glaze.

3 Cut the sugar paste in half. Knead a little food coloring into each. On a work surface dusted with confectioners' sugar, roll out each piece into a strip about 3x12in (7x30cm). Wrap neatly around the flat sides of the cubes.

4 Gradually beat the sugar into the egg white until smooth. Spoon into a small paper pastry bag (see page 144) and snip a tiny piece off the end to make a very small hole. Pipe the door and windows on one side of each cake. Arrange the chocolates over the tops as tiles.

 Oven temperature
325°F/160°C

 Baking time
1 hour

 Cake pan
8x4x2½in (20x10x6cm) loaf pan, greased and lined

 Makes
2 houses

 Storage
Keep for 1–2 days, undecorated or 3–4 days decorated

 Freezing
Freeze for 1 month, undecorated

 Step ahead
Make the apricot glaze; make and color the sugar paste

Porcupine Cake

This appealing cake is very easy to make. A light and fudgy sponge, made by the all-in-one method, is covered with chocolate icing and decorated with chocolate quills. Make and decorate the cake a couple of days ahead of time to allow the flavors to develop. (See page 29 for illustration.)

INGREDIENTS

For the cake

1½ cups (200g) self-rising flour

scant 1 cup (200g) granulated sugar

½ cup (125g) butter, softened

2 eggs

2 tbsp cocoa powder

5 tbsp (75ml) evaporated milk

5 tbsp (75ml) water

For the icing and decoration

1¼ cups (300ml) heavy cream

3½ oz (100g) semisweet chocolate, finely grated

12 imported chocolate flake bars, or about 24 reception sticks, broken

4oz (125g) marzipan, colored with a drop of brown food coloring

1 red chocolate candy

2 chocolate chips

1 For the cake, put all the ingredients in a bowl and beat together until light and fluffy. Spoon into the prepared Pyrex mold, place on a baking sheet, and bake in the preheated oven for 1 hour, or until a skewer inserted into the cake comes out clean. Remove from the oven and let rest for about 5 minutes. Invert onto a wire rack and let cool.

2 For the icing, bring the cream slowly to a boil. Immediately remove from the heat and stir in the grated chocolate. Mix well, let cool, and then chill for 1–3 hours, until very thick and spreadable.

3 Cut each flake bar roughly into four lengthwise. Cut each one into thin 1in (2.5cm) "quills." The pieces do not have to be regular or even in shape.

4 Trim the base of the cake level so that it sits flat and place cut side down on a cutting board. Cut in half vertically. Spread a little of the chocolate icing on each side of the flat base and press both iced sides together to make the porcupine's body. Place on a cake board or large plate.

TO FINISH THE CAKE

Mold the marzipan into a small cone shape for the porcupine's face. Attach it to one end of the body with a little of the icing. Spread the rest of the icing all over the body. Starting at the back of the porcupine, push the "quills" into the icing at a slight angle, saving the smallest pieces for the area at the front around the face. Using a little more icing, attach the red chocolate candy to the tip of the cone for the nose and the chocolate chips for the eyes. Chill for 2 hours to set the icing before serving.

 Oven temperature
350°F/180°C

 Baking time
1 hour

 Cake mold
4-cup (900ml) round-bottomed Pyrex mold, greased and base-lined with a small circle of waxed paper

 Makes
16 slices

 Storage
Keeps for 3–4 days

 Freezing
Freezes for 1 month, undecorated

Teddy Bear Cake

A cake for teddy bear devotees. Plain and chocolate genoise sponges, made with half the amount of butter to give a less rich cake, are filled with a layer of jam, shaped into a teddy bear, and decorated with brightly colored sugar paste. To make a very simple version, just make one 9in (23cm) square sponge and cover with buttercream. Then instead of making a teddy-shaped cake, simply use the template (see page 157) to cut out the various shapes from colored sugar paste and place them on the cake.

INGREDIENTS

For the plain cake

6 tbsp (90g) unsalted butter
¾ cup (180g) granulated sugar
6 eggs
1¼ cups (180g) all-purpose flour
1½ tsp finely grated lemon zest

For the chocolate cake

1 cup plus 2 tbsp (150g) all-purpose flour
¼ cup (30g) cocoa powder
6 tbsp (90g) butter
¾ cup (180g) granulated sugar
6 eggs

For the decoration

one 11in (28cm) square cake board
2½lb (1.25kg) sugar paste (see page 152)
1¼ yards (1.15 meters) blue ribbon
6 tbsp (90ml) apricot jam
1 quantity simple buttercream (see page 150)
yellow, blue, red, and green food coloring paste
4 tbsp apricot glaze (see page 155)
3 small balloons
3 short pieces narrow colored ribbon

1 Make the plain cake (see Rich Genoise Sponge page 67 for the method). Pour into the prepared pan and bake in the preheated oven for 20–25 minutes, or until a skewer comes out clean. Remove from the oven and let rest for 5 minutes. Invert onto a wire rack, peel off the lining paper, and let cool. For the chocolate cake, sift the flour with the cocoa and follow the same method.

2 Cover the cake board with 8oz (250g) sugar paste (see page 141). Trim the edge of the board with the blue ribbon and let dry for 2–3 hours.

3 Cut each cake horizontally in half. Sandwich one plain cake layer between two chocolate layers using the apricot jam. Spread a thin layer of the simple buttercream over the whole cake. On a surface dusted with confectioners' sugar, roll out 1lb (500g) sugar paste into a 14in (35cm) square and use to cover the cake (see page 141). Position the cake in the middle of the board. Save a small piece of white sugar paste for the eye.

4 Trace the bear shape and a number onto waxed paper (see page 156) and cut out. Use this template to cut the remaining plain cake into a bear shape. Cut the cake trimmings into small squares to form presents.

5 Color 5oz (150g) of the sugar paste yellow. Divide the rest into three and color blue, red, and green. Brush the bear with apricot glaze. Roll out the yellow sugar paste and cover the bear. Reroll the trimmings and cut out the top leg shape and a number using the template. Shape a small piece for the nose and roll the remainder into thin ribbons for the presents.

6 Make the eye from the reserved white and a little blue sugar paste. Attach the leg, nose, ears, and eye with a little water. Mark the fingers and mouth with a skewer.

7 Roll out the blue sugar paste and cut out the sweater using the template. Roll another piece into a thin rope and use to trim the number. Shape a little red icing into a bow tie and 20 small dots and place on the bear. Use the remaining icing to cover the presents, and use the trimmings for ribbons and bows.

8 Position the bear, a few of the presents, and the number on the cake as shown. Give away any remaining presents as party favors. Tie the balloons with the ribbon. Secure to the bear's hand with water and sugar paste.

 Oven temperature
350°F/180°C

 Baking time
20–25 minutes for each cake

 Cake pan
9in (23cm) deep, square pan, greased and lined

 Makes
25 slices

 Storage
Keeps for 1 week

 Freezing
Sponges freeze for 1 month, undecorated

 Step ahead
Make the sugar paste, cover the cake board and let dry for 2–3 hours; make the simple buttercream and apricot glaze

Ribbon & Candle Cake

Some years ago a friend of mine held a birthday party for her daughter, Elizabeth, in a park. Each child was given a picnic basket filled with a tempting selection of little sandwiches, potato chips, and fruit. The birthday cake for dessert was a large, moist square of delicious carrot, almond, and orange cake covered with cream cheese frosting and colorfully bedecked with candles and ribbons. The children loved it. (See page 28 for illustration.)

INGREDIENTS

For the cake

1¼ cups (250g) cake flour, sifted

2 tsp baking powder

½ tsp baking soda

pinch of salt

1–1½ tsp ground cinnamon

1¼ cups (300g) peeled and grated carrots, patted dry with paper towels

1 cup (125g) ground almonds

1¼ cups (250g) light brown sugar

3 eggs

finely grated zest of 1 orange

½ cup (125g) butter, melted and cooled

For the decoration

2 quantities cream cheese frosting (see page 150)

one sturdy 12in (30cm) cake board

one large sheet pink paper

1¼ yards (1.15 meters) matching pink ribbon for the edge of the board

6 ivory taper candles

2½ yards (2.3 meters) narrow pink ribbon

1¼ yards (1.15 metres) wide dark pink ribbon

1 Make the cake following the recipe for the Carrot and Hazelnut Loaf (see page 89 for the method). Pour into the prepared pan and bake in the preheated oven for 30 minutes, or until a skewer inserted into the cake comes out clean. Remove from the oven and invert onto a wire rack. Peel off the lining paper and let cool.

2 Cover the cake board with the paper and trim the edge with the ribbon. Cut off each corner of the cake at an angle to make an octagon, so that each of the eight sides measures 4in (10 cm). Position the cake on the board. Spread two thirds of the frosting evenly over the top and sides of the cake.

3 Spoon the remaining frosting into a pastry bag fitted with a ½in (1cm) star nozzle and pipe in a shell design (see page 145) around the base and top edge of the cake. Chill for 30 minutes.

4 Cut the candles to the desired length. Wrap short pieces of the narrow ribbons around the candles and arrange in the center of the cake. Put the dark ribbon around the cake.

 Oven temperature
350°F/180°C

 Baking time
30 minutes

 Cake pan
9in (23cm) deep, square pan, greased and lined

 Makes
18 slices

 Storage
Let mature for 2–3 days; keeps for 1–2 days once decorated

 Freezing
Freezes for 1 month, undecorated

 Step ahead
Make the cream cheese frosting; cover the cake board and prepare the candles

4

Icings, Fillings, & Decorations

It is the finishing touches that often make a cake memorable. Here, clearly illustrated instructions show how to achieve a professional look, whether applying the simplest dusting of confectioners' sugar, sugar-frosting fresh flowers, or piping a decorative icing. There are also key recipes for a selection of buttercreams, icings, and other luxurious finishes and elegant decorations.

Icings & Other Finishes

A covering of icing can turn a simple cake into a luxurious centerpiece. Cakes for special occasions are often covered in sugar paste. Rich fruit cakes need a layer of marzipan first.

If the top of the cake is not flat, start by leveling it with a separate circle of marzipan. Sponge cakes can be given a softer finish with glacé icing or buttercream.

COVERING IN MARZIPAN (see page 152; instructions below for an 8in/20cm round fruit cake)

1 Brush the cake with apricot glaze. To level the top, roll out 8oz (250g) marzipan into a circle just larger than the cake's diameter. Invert the cake onto it and press the excess into any gaps.

2 Transfer the cake to a 10in (25cm) round cake board, top side up. To cover the whole cake with a layer of marzipan, measure across the top and down the sides with a piece of string.

3 Place 1½ lb (750g) marzipan on a surface dusted with confectioners' sugar. Roll out with a long, narrow rolling pin into a large circle, using the piece of string as a guide.

4 Brush the marzipan top with a little brandy. Using the rolling pin, lift the circle of marzipan over the cake and press smoothly onto the top and sides. Neatly trim off the excess at the base.

5 Let the surface dry out in a cool, dry place for at least 24 hours. When ready to cover the cake with sugar paste, brush the marzipan surface with brandy or boiled water once more.

Moistening the marzipan helps sugar paste stick

Brushing with brandy adds rich flavor

COVERING IN SUGAR PASTE (see page 152)

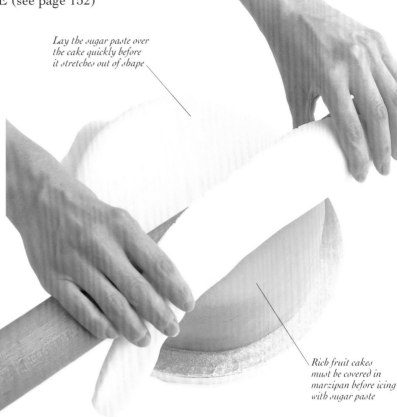

Lay the sugar paste over the cake quickly before it stretches out of shape

Rich fruit cakes must be covered in marzipan before icing with sugar paste

1 Measure the depth and diameter of the cake with string as step 2 opposite. Knead the sugar paste until smooth. Roll out into a circle on a surface dusted with confectioners' sugar, using the string as a guide. Gently lift it over the rolling pin.

2 Carefully lift the sugar paste. With one edge touching the board nearest to you, drape it over the moistened surface of the cake and let it fall neatly down the other side. Gently smooth it onto the top and sides of the cake.

3 Dip your fingers in cornstarch or confectioners' sugar and smooth away any creases. For a finer finish, rub the icing lightly with a cake smoother.

4 Neatly trim away the excess icing at the bottom with a small, sharp knife. Carefully run a narrow spatula under the cake and lift it off the board.

5 Roll out 8oz (250g) sugar paste into a circle a little larger than the board. Brush the board with apricot glaze (see page 149). Lay the icing over it and trim.

6 Carefully replace the cake in the center of the board without damaging the sugar paste. Cover the edge of the board with a ribbon to give a neat finish, and decorate the top of the cake as desired.

HANDY TIP

◆ *Before icing with sugar paste, cover rich fruit cakes with marzipan to prevent the color of the cake from staining the icing. Coat sponge cakes with apricot glaze or a little buttercream.*

Icing Sponge Cakes

Choose flavorings that complement the cake: buttercreams enhance rich cakes; plainer cakes can be finished with a simple glacé icing or just a dusting of confectioners' sugar.

GLACE ICING (see page 152)

1 Place the cake on a wire rack set over a tray or large plate to catch the excess icing. Brush the surface of the cake with apricot glaze if specified in the recipe and let stand for 2–3 minutes until set. Pour the icing onto the center of the cake.

BUTTERCREAM (see page 150)

2 As the icing starts to spread out, coax it gently over the top and down the sides of the cake with a narrow spatula, so that it coats the whole surface in a smooth, even layer.

3 Let the icing set and then carefully transfer the cake to a serving plate. Decorate as desired.

HANDY TIP

♦ *It is important to get the consistency of glacé icing just right. If too liquid, it will run off, and if too thick, it will not give a smooth finish.*

1 Place the cake on a wire rack. Make sure the buttercream is at room temperature. Spread it in an even layer over the top of the cake with a narrow spatula, using a paddling action.

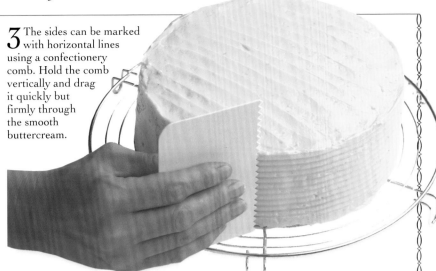

3 The sides can be marked with horizontal lines using a confectionery comb. Hold the comb vertically and drag it quickly but firmly through the smooth buttercream.

2 Spread a layer of buttercream over the sides of the cake using the narrow spatula. Make sure the layer is generous and even.

FINISHING THE SIDES OF A CAKE

To decorate a cake's side with grated chocolate or chopped nuts, balance the covered cake on the palm of one hand. Hold it over a plate of coating. Lift the coating onto the sides of the cake using a large narrow spatula, pressing gently so that the coating stays in place.

The decorated sides

GLAZING A FRUIT TART

Give cakes and desserts covered in fresh fruit an attractive glossy finish by carefully spooning over a thin, even layer of a jam-based glaze (see page 149), making sure all the fruit is completely covered.

DUSTING IN CONFECTIONERS' SUGAR

Place the cold cake on a wire rack and spoon a little confectioners' sugar into a fine-mesh sieve or sifter. Hold it about 3in (7cm) above the cake and tap the side, moving it a little each time, to give a light, even dusting.

Piping Methods

A decorative design of piped icing or whipped cream can transform the simplest cake into something quite stunning. For more liquid icings and melted chocolate, it is best to work with small amounts using a homemade paper pastry bag. A nylon pastry bag fitted with a piping nozzle is better for larger quantities of whipped cream and thicker buttercreams.

MAKING A PAPER PASTRY BAG

1 Unroll a length of waxed paper. Fold one corner of the paper across to meet the opposite corner of an imaginary square. Crease and cut along the fold to remove a triangle of paper.

2 Fold the triangle in half to make a smaller triangle. Place it on a flat surface with the longest side facing vertically toward you. Bring the top point down to meet the middle one.

3 Fold the paper down twice to meet the bottom point. Open up into a cone. Turn over the edge above the seam to secure (see inset). Snip off the tip, fill, and fold over the top to seal.

FILLING A NYLON PASTRY BAG

1 Drop a nozzle into the bag, pushing it to the end so no gaps are left. Hold the bag halfway up and fold back the excess fabric. Half fill, pushing the icing or cream down to remove air pockets.

2 Unfold the fabric and tightly twist just above the filling. Hold upright, with one hand firmly holding the twisted top and the other placed more lightly farther down to guide the piping.

3 Squeeze from the top of the pastry bag with a firm and even pressure, retwisting the bag as it empties, so that the remaining space always stays full. Refill when necessary.

PIPED DESIGNS

Hold the bag next to, but not quite touching, the surface of the cake as you work. Apply even pressure when piping and always stop squeezing before removing the bag. For most designs you will need a ½ in (1cm) star nozzle. For basketweave, fit one paper pastry bag with a ¹⁄₁₆ in (1.25mm) plain writing or star nozzle, and a second paper pastry bag with a ½ in (1cm) ribbon nozzle.

  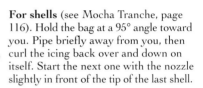

For small stars (see Esterházy Cream Torte, page 71). Hold the bag upright. Squeeze out a small mound of icing without twisting the bag.

For rosettes (see Dobos Torta, page 74). Hold the bag upright. Use a circular motion to form a swirl with a peak.

½ in (1cm)
star nozzle

For shells (see Mocha Tranche, page 116). Hold the bag at a 95° angle toward you. Pipe briefly away from you, then curl the icing back over and down on itself. Start the next one with the nozzle slightly in front of the tip of the last shell.

For a rope (see Gâteau St. Honoré, page 76). Hold the bag at a 95° angle toward you. Pipe in a continuous movement, twisting the icing into a tight spiral.

½ in (1cm)
ribbon nozzle

For basketweave (see Autumn Wedding Cake, page 124). Pipe vertical lines with the star or writing nozzle, about ½ in (1cm) apart, over the surface of the cake. With the ribbon nozzle at the top edge or bottom of the cake, pipe a short horizontal strip of icing over the outermost vertical line, up to the next line. Continue over every alternate line. Pipe a second strip of horizontal icing alongside the first, starting at the second vertical line in. Repeat to cover.

¹⁄₁₆ in (1.25mm)
star nozzle

For chocolate fans (see Orange and Chocolate Layer Cake, page 81). Spoon melted chocolate into a paper pastry bag. Seal and snip off the tip. Pipe fans onto a baking sheet lined with baking parchment. When set, gently lift off.

Paper pastry bag
with tip cut off

Decorating with Chocolate

Chocolate gives an elegant finish to all types of cakes and cookies. It can be melted (see page 44) and used simply as is, incorporated into more luxurious icings, or made into small, individual decorations. Refrigerate chocolate-covered cakes, cookies, and decorations briefly to help them set, then avoid touching them as chocolate marks and melts very easily.

MAKING CHOCOLATE CARAQUE

1 Spread 4oz (125g) melted chocolate on a scratch-proof surface in a thin, even layer with a narrow spatula. Leave at room temperature until dry and set.

2 Hold both ends of a large, sharp knife at a 45° angle. Pull it gently across the chocolate's surface so that the chocolate rolls up into long curls.

Chocolate caraque

COATING COOKIES IN CHOCOLATE

Spread the underside of each cookie with an even layer of melted chocolate using a small, round-bladed knife. Let set very slightly. Mark the chocolate surface with a wavy design using a fork. Let set, chocolate side up, on a rack before serving or storing.

Florentine cookies

MAKING CHOCOLATE LEAVES

1 Choose nontoxic leaves such as rose, violet, or mint. Rinse and dry well before using. With a small, clean pastry brush, coat the underside of each leaf with a thin layer of melted chocolate.

2 When the first layer has set, coat once more. Chill in the refrigerator for a few minutes. Carefully peel the leaves away from the chocolate, being careful not to touch it too much.

Chocolate rose leaves

Pour the icing onto the center of the cake

COVERING A CAKE IN RICH CHOCOLATE ICING

This is the classic icing for Sacher Torte (see page 83), but it can also be used to cover other chocolate and sponge cakes. Let the icing set in a cool place before slicing the cake.

1 Pour scant 1 cup (200ml) heavy cream into a pan, place over low heat, and bring slowly to a boil. Remove from the heat, add 6oz (180g) finely grated semisweet chocolate and stir well until melted. Let cool and thicken slightly, stirring occasionally. Use while still warm and liquid.

2 Place the cake on a rack over a plate. Pour the icing onto the cake. Tilt the rack until the cake is covered in a smooth, even layer. Let set, then transfer to a serving plate. The icing will stay glossy for about 24 hours.

MAKING CHOCOLATE CURLS

Use at room temperature

Bring a bar of chocolate to room temperature. Using a sharp, swivel-bladed vegetable peeler, shave small curls from the sides of the bar.

GRATING CHOCOLATE

Chill the chocolate in the freezer for a short time before using to prevent the chocolate from sticking to the grater. Grate on the largest holes, using a grater or a food processor.

Cake Decorations

It is the attention to small finishing details that gives a cake an attractive, professional appearance. This requires a little extra time and patience but no particular skill. Some decorations can be prepared in advance, then arranged on the cake when needed. Flowers have a much shorter life, so leave them in plenty of water in a cool place before using and prepare them as near to the time as possible.

FRESH FLOWER DECORATIONS

Simplicity is elegance, and flowers, with their fleeting freshness, transform the plainest cake into an exciting and sumptuous confection. Choose flowers that are safe to use with food, preferably garden grown and not sprayed with chemicals. Select those with strong stems and thick petals such as roses and rose buds, carnations, violas and pansies, sweet peas, nasturtiums, and day lilies.

SUGAR-FROSTED FLOWERS

1 Cut off the flower head, leaving a short stem attached. With a small, clean pastry brush, carefully coat each petal as evenly as possible with a thin layer of lightly beaten egg white.

2 Spoon a little superfine sugar between each petal, making sure each one is well coated, and then shake out the excess sugar. Carefully push the stems through a wire rack and let dry.

MARZIPAN CARROTS

Knead 2oz (60g) white marzipan until smooth. Knead in a little orange food coloring powder or liquid until you reach the required shade. Divide the marzipan into 16 even-sized pieces and roll between your fingers into small carrot shapes. Mark each one with ridges using a toothpick. Cut a piece of angelica into small strips and push one into the fatter end of each carrot to make a stalk.

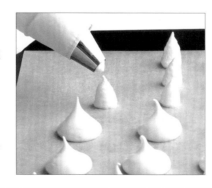

FROSTED GRAPES

Separate the grapes from the stem. Dip one at a time into unbeaten egg white, then spoon on superfine sugar to coat. Let dry on baking parchment.

MERINGUE MUSHROOMS

1 Whisk 1 egg white into soft peaks. Gradually whisk in ¼ cup (60g) superfine sugar to make a stiff, glossy meringue. Spoon into a pastry bag fitted with a ¼in (5mm) plain nozzle.

2 For the caps, pipe twenty 1in (2.5cm) mounds on a lined baking sheet. Pipe the remainder into twenty small high-peaked stems. Bake in the oven at 300°F/150°C for ¾ hour. Remove and let cool. Make a small hole in the bottom of each cap with a fine skewer.

3 Melt 1oz (30g) chocolate (see page 44) and spread over the underside of each cap. Push the stems, point first, into the holes. Let set on their sides.

Fruit Preparations

The addition of fruit often enriches the quality of a cake. The zest of sharp, citric lemons and oranges enhances the flavor and adds a fine aroma and color. Fruit-preserve glazes, richly sweet and yet tart, have a sticky texture that helps to bond the surface and add taste, as well as giving a glistening sheen to fresh fruit toppings. Cooked fruit lends moisture to drier cake mixtures.

COARSE LEMON ZEST

Drag a citrus zester (see page 39) firmly across the outside of a scrubbed or unwaxed lemon, taking care not to remove any of the bitter white pith that lies just underneath the colored zest.

FINE LEMON SHREDS

Remove the zest from a lemon in strips using a peeler, taking care not to remove any pith. Cut into fine shreds. Blanch in boiling water for 30 seconds. Drain, refresh in cold water, and drain again.

RASPBERRY SAUCE

Put ½ pint (250g) raspberries and 2 tablespoons confectioners' sugar in a bowl. Crush into a rough purée. Press through a sieve and then chill.

Sieve the raspberries to remove the seeds

APPLE PUREE

Cook 2 medium peeled, cored, and sliced cooking apples with ⅓ cup (60g) brown sugar and 1 tablespoon water. Cook for 10–15 minutes, until soft. Press through a sieve, cover, and let cool.

PUMPKIN PUREE

Cut 2lb (1kg) fresh pumpkin into wedges. Peel and scoop out the seeds. Put in a steamer or colander resting over a pan of simmering water. Steam for 15–20 minutes, until soft. Cool slightly, then press through a fine sieve. Cover and let stand until cold.

RED CURRANT GLAZE

Put 3–4 tablespoons red currant jelly and 2–3 teaspoons water or kirsch into a small pan and let stand over low heat until the jelly has melted and is completely clear. Let cool until slightly thickened but use while still warm. This glaze covers a 9in (23cm) fruit tart.

APRICOT GLAZE

Put 1 cup (125g) apricot jam and 3 tablespoons water in a small pan and let stand over gentle heat until the jam has melted. Pour into a sieve over a small bowl and press through with a wooden spoon. Keeps in the refrigerator, in a sterilized screw-top jar, for 2 weeks. Warm it before use.

Fillings, Icings, & Toppings

The flavor of a cake is often enhanced by the addition of a light cream filling and a delicious decorative topping. Here are key recipes for creams, icings, and toppings used throughout the book. Always allow plenty of time for their preparation as they often benefit from chilling before use. Remember to remove rings before you work with marzipan and sugar paste.

SIMPLE BUTTERCREAM

INGREDIENTS

½ cup (125g) unsalted butter, softened
2 cups (250g) confectioners' sugar, sifted
1 tsp vanilla extract or other flavoring (optional)
1 tbsp cream or milk

Put the softened butter in a bowl and gradually beat in the confectioners' sugar until the mixture is pale and creamy. Beat in the vanilla extract or other flavoring and the cream or milk to give a spreading consistency.

CHESTNUT BUTTERCREAM

INGREDIENTS

½ cup (125g) unsalted butter, softened
½ cup (60g) confectioners' sugar, sifted
½ cup (125g) unsweetened chestnut purée (available in specialty stores)
1 tbsp dark rum

Beat the butter and confectioners' sugar together until the mixture is pale and fluffy. Then beat in the chestnut purée, a spoonful at a time. Mix in the rum. Chill for 30 minutes before using.

CREAM CHEESE FROSTING

INGREDIENTS

4oz (125g) cream cheese
1½ cups (190g) confectioners' sugar, sifted
1 egg white, slightly beaten
½ tsp vanilla extract

Beat the cream cheese, confectioners' sugar, and egg white together until smooth. Then add the vanilla extract. Do not overbeat: the frosting thickens slightly as you spread it.

MOUSSELINE BUTTERCREAM

This is a firm, smooth buttercream that holds its shape even in warm conditions. To make sure it spreads smoothly, bring back to room temperature before using.

INGREDIENTS

⅓ cup (75g) granulated sugar
3 egg yolks
¾ cup (180g) unsalted butter, softened
1 tsp vanilla extract

HANDY TIPS

- *The egg yolk mixture must be cool before it is added to the butter or the butter will melt.*
- *This buttercream will keep refrigerated for 4–5 days, or can be frozen for up to 1 month.*

1 Gently heat the granulated sugar and 4 tablespoons cold water in a small heavy-bottomed pan until dissolved. Bring to a boil and boil to the soft ball stage at 240°F/115°C (see page 153).

2 In another bowl, lightly whisk the egg yolks. Gradually pour in the hot syrup, whisking vigorously all the time. Continue whisking for about 5 minutes, until the mixture is pale, thick, and cool.

3 Beat the butter until pale and creamy. Gradually beat in spoonfuls of the cooled egg and sugar mixture. Beat in the vanilla extract. Chill in the refrigerator for at least 30 minutes.

VARIATIONS
Coffee: Dissolve 2 tbsp instant coffee in 1 tbsp boiling water. Cool, then beat into the basic mixture.

Chocolate: Melt 3½oz (100g) semisweet chocolate. Let cool, then beat in.
Liqueur: Beat in 1–2 tbsp dark rum, kirsch, Grand Marnier, or Cointreau.

Lemon: Beat in 1 tbsp lemon juice and the finely grated zest of 1 lemon.
Orange: Beat in 1 tbsp orange juice and the finely grated zest of 1 orange.

CHOCOLATE GANACHE

This is a smooth, rich, and quite delicious unsweetened chocolate cream. The ganache is cooked, and then cooled for 1–1½ hours, but must be used while still soft because it hardens once cold. For a fresh vanilla flavor, first infuse a 2in (5cm) piece of vanilla bean in the cream. Remove the bean before adding the grated chocolate. This quantity of ganache is sufficient to cover a 9in (23cm) cake.

INGREDIENTS

1¼ cups (300ml) heavy cream
2½ oz (75g) semisweet chocolate, finely grated

1 Pour the cream into a small pan and slowly bring to a boil over gentle heat. Take the cream off the heat and gradually stir in the grated chocolate until well incorporated.

2 Refrigerate until firm but not set. Beat well until the mixture is paler in color.

─── HANDY TIP ───
◆ *In warm weather the chocolate quantity can be increased slightly to give a firmer set.*

QUICK CHOCOLATE BUTTERCREAM

INGREDIENTS

1 tsp instant coffee
1 tsp cocoa powder
2oz (60g) semisweet chocolate, broken into pieces
1 cup (250g) unsalted butter, softened
½ cup (75g) confectioners' sugar, sifted

1 Dissolve the instant coffee and cocoa powder in 2 tablespoons boiling water. Pour into a small heatproof bowl, add the chocolate pieces, and melt over a small pan of simmering water, stirring occasionally. Let cool until thickened but not set.

2 In another bowl, beat the butter and confectioners' sugar together until pale and fluffy. Add the chocolate and stir in until well combined. Then beat the mixture until it becomes pale, fluffy, and thick. This will keep refrigerated in a sealed container for up to 1 week.

CREME PATISSIERE

Crème pâtissière, or pastry cream, is a rich, custardlike mixture used to fill sweet tarts and pastries. It is much thicker than normal custard. This prevents the pastry bottom of fruit tarts from becoming soggy and enables them to be sliced neatly. It can also be piped successfully.

─── HANDY TIPS ───
◆ *Crème pâtissière can be thinned by folding in a little lightly whipped cream once it is cold if you wish.*

◆ *It will keep for up to 2 days in the refrigerator.*

INGREDIENTS

1 cup plus 2 tbsp (275ml) milk
¼ of a vanilla bean or ½ tsp vanilla extract
3 egg yolks
3 tbsp superfine sugar
1½ tbsp all-purpose flour
1½ tbsp cornstarch
3 tbsp heavy cream

1 Bring the milk to a boil in a small pan. If you are using a vanilla bean, add it to the milk and set aside for about 30 minutes to infuse.

2 Put the egg yolks in a small heatproof bowl. Add the sugar and beat until slightly pale and creamy. Sift the flour and cornstarch over the egg yolk mixture and beat together well until the mixture becomes smooth.

3 Remove the vanilla bean and bring the milk back to a boil. Pour onto the egg yolk mixture and mix carefully. Return to the pan and bring to a boil, stirring vigorously. Simmer for 2 minutes, stirring, until smooth and thick.

4 Stir in the vanilla extract, if using, and the cream. Pour into a bowl and press plastic wrap or waxed paper onto the surface. Let cool and then chill for 2 hours before using.

MARZIPAN

Use to cover celebration cakes and for smaller decorations. This recipe makes 1lb (500g), enough to cover a 7in (18cm) fruit cake.

INGREDIENTS

1 cup (125g) confectioners' sugar, sifted

½ cup (125g) superfine sugar

2 cups (250g) ground almonds

1 tsp lemon juice

few drops of almond extract (optional)

2 egg whites

Mix the sugars and almonds in a bowl. Add the lemon juice, almond extract, and enough egg white to make a soft dough. Knead on a surface dusted with confectioners' sugar, until smooth. Cover with plastic wrap until needed.

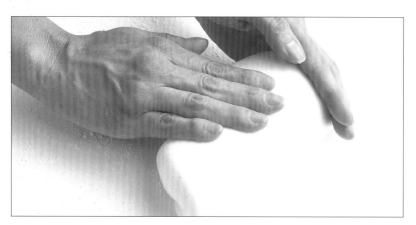

SUGAR PASTE

Also known as fondant icing, this is used to decorate novelty cakes and wedding cakes. It is simple to make and gives a smooth, professional finish. This recipe makes 1lb (500g) sugar paste, sufficient to cover an 8in (20cm) cake. To color the icing, add very small quantities of food coloring, and knead in until it is evenly distributed throughout the sugar paste. **Warning this recipe contains raw egg (see page 9).**

INGREDIENTS

3½ cups (425g) confectioners' sugar, sifted

1 egg white

1 tbsp corn syrup

1 Sift the sugar into a bowl. Add the egg white and corn syrup, and gradually stir together with a small round-bladed knife until it starts to stick together in lumps. Knead the pieces together in the bowl to form a ball.

2 Turn the mixture out onto a surface dusted with confectioners' sugar. Knead for about 10 minutes, until the paste is very smooth, dusting the surface with more sugar to prevent it from sticking. Cover tightly with plastic wrap, and keep in an airtight container in the refrigerator until needed.

PROCESSOR METHOD
Sift the sugar into the bowl of a food processor. Add the egg white and corn syrup and process until it forms a smooth ball. Knead gently to blend.

GLACE ICING

This simple icing is best on light textured cakes and pastries and is used while still warm. Iced cakes keep for only a few days before the icing starts to crack. The quantity here is sufficient to cover the top and sides of an 8–8½ in (20–22cm) round cake.

INGREDIENTS

1¼ cups (200g) confectioners' sugar, sifted

7–8 tsp boiling water

4 drops of vanilla extract

1 Sift the sugar into a small bowl. Gradually stir in the boiling water until the mixture is smooth and coats the back of a spoon. If too thin it will soak into the cake; if too thick it will not spread. Adjust with sugar or water. Stir in the vanilla extract.

2 Rest the bowl over a small pan of simmering water and leave for 1–2 minutes until warm. Use immediately.

VARIATIONS
To color the icing: Dip the tip of a fine skewer into liquid or paste food coloring. Stir in until evenly colored.

To flavor the icing: Make as for the main recipe, omitting the vanilla extract and substituting the following liquids for the water:
Orange: 2 tbsp strained fresh orange juice and 1–2 tsp strained lemon juice.
Lemon: 7–8 tsp strained lemon juice.
Liqueur: 7–8 tsp spirit (such as dark rum, Cointreau, kirsch).
Coffee: Dissolve 1 tbsp instant coffee in 1 tsp boiling water, plus 6–7 tsp additional boiling water.
Chocolate: Replace ¼ cup (30g) of the confectioners' sugar with ¼ cup (30g) cocoa powder. Sift together, then gradually add 7–8 tsp boiling water.

BOILED SUGAR SYRUP

When sugar and water are boiled, a syrup forms. The more concentrated and hotter the syrup becomes, the darker and thicker it will be and the harder it will set. A "soft ball" syrup is used instead of sugar for making mousseline buttercream, and caramel can be used for decorating elaborate cakes. Adding cream of tartar prevents the syrup from crystallizing.

INGREDIENTS

pinch of cream of tartar

⅔ cup (150ml) cold water

2½ cups (500g) granulated sugar

1 Mix the cream of tartar with about 1 teaspoon of the water. Pour the rest into a heavy-bottomed pan. Put the sugar into the center and heat gently until it has dissolved and the liquid is clear.

2 Stir in the dissolved cream of tartar. Increase the heat and bring to a boil. Stand a candy thermometer in the pan and boil the syrup rapidly to the required temperature (see above).

SIMPLE SUGAR SYRUP

This is a basic stock syrup that can be made in advance and stored in the refrigerator as a base for flavored syrups to moisten layer cakes.

INGREDIENTS

½ cup (125ml) water

1 cup (200g) granulated or superfine sugar

3 Take the pan off the heat and plunge the bottom into cold water to stop the syrup from cooking further. Use immediately.

Soft Ball: Boil the syrup for about 1 minute, until it reaches 240°F (115°C). If you drop a little of the syrup into a glass of cold water, then knead it between your fingers, it should form a soft ball.

Caramel: Boil the syrup for about 7 minutes, until it reaches 345°F (173°C) and turns a rich amber color. Be careful; if cooked for too long it will burn.

Warm the candy thermometer before using

Do not stir the sugar syrup at all during boiling

Place the water and sugar in a heavy-bottomed pan. Leave over low heat, stirring constantly, until the sugar has completely dissolved and the liquid is clear. Bring the liquid to a rolling boil and immediately remove the pan from the heat. Leave the syrup until absolutely cold and then pour it into a sterilized jar and seal well. Keep refrigerated until needed; it will keep almost indefinitely.

VARIATIONS

Liqueur syrup: Mix 1 tbsp Cointreau, Grand Marnier, dark rum, Tia Maria or kirsch with 2 tbsp syrup.

Rum and citrus syrup: Stir ½ tsp each of finely grated orange and lemon zest into 6 tbsp warm syrup. Leave for 10 minutes. Strain and mix with 3 tbsp dark rum.

Coffee syrup: Dissolve 1 tbsp instant coffee in 1 tsp boiling water. Cool and mix with 1 tbsp syrup.

What Went Wrong?

WHISKED & SEPARATED EGG MIXTURES

Why is the cake's texture dense and heavy?

► The eggs were too small.
► Insufficient air was whisked into the egg and sugar mixture.
► The flour was not folded in gently by hand using a large metal spoon.
► The melted butter was too hot when added, causing it to sink down through the whisked foam.
► The oven temperature was too low.

Why has the top of the cake dropped?

► The oven temperature was too hot.
► The cake was not cooked long enough.
► The cake pan was bumped during baking.
► The oven door was opened too soon, which created a draft.

Why did the jelly roll crack while being rolled?

► The sponge was overcooked so it was too dry.
► The mixture was not spread out evenly in the baking tray, causing some parts to overcook and dry out before the rest of the sponge.
► The crisp edges of the cooked sponge were not trimmed away before rolling.
► The sponge was left for too long before rolling.

BLENDED & CREAMED MIXTURES

Why has the mixture curdled?

► The ingredients were not at room temperature.
► The butter and sugar were not creamed together well enough before adding the eggs.
► The eggs were added too quickly.

Why is the cake's texture heavy?

► The butter, sugar, and eggs were not beaten together long enough.
► The flour was stirred in too vigorously, therefore knocking out the air incorporated during creaming.
► Too much flour was added to the creamed mixture.

► The baking powder was left out.
► The oven temperature was not hot enough.

Why has the cake peaked and cracked?

► The oven temperature was too hot, causing the outside of the cake to bake and form a crust too quickly. As the mixture in the center of the cake continued to cook and rise, it burst up through the top of the cake.
► The cake was on too high a shelf in the oven.

Why has the dried fruit sunk in the cake?

► The pieces of fruit were too large and too heavy.
► The sugary syrup on the outside of the glacé fruit was not washed off; this caused the pieces of fruit to slide through the mixture as it heated.
► The washed and dried fruit was not dusted with flour before being added to the mixture.
► The cake mixture was overbeaten or too wet so it could not hold the fruit in place.
► The oven temperature was too low, causing the mixture to melt before it set to hold the fruit in place.

GENERAL

Why did the cake rise unevenly in the oven?

► The flour was not blended sufficiently into the main mixture.
► The sides of the pan were greased unevenly.
► The temperature inside the oven was uneven.
► The oven temperature was too high.

Why did the mixture overflow in the oven?

► The size of the cake pan recommended in the recipe was not used. The uncooked mixture should fill the pan by no more than two-thirds.

Why was the cake overcooked and the top burned?

► All the recipes in the book have been baked in a conventional oven. Convection ovens bake more quickly, so the temperature will need to be adjusted. Refer to the manufacturer's handbook.

► Rich fruit cakes usually require longer baking, so they should be covered with foil halfway through the cooking process.

Why was the cake burned on the bottom?

► A poor-quality pan was used. Usually too thin, they can develop hot spots and warp in the oven.

► The cake was baked near the bottom of the oven.

Why are there holes in the baked cake?

► The pan with the raw whisked cake mixture was not rapped on the work surface before baking.

Why did small brown speckles appear on the surface of the cake or cookies?

► Granulated sugar sometimes does not dissolve fully. Try using superfine sugar.

PASTRY

Why did the pastry shrink away from the sides of the tart pan during baking?

► The pastry was stretched while it was rolled out.

► The pastry was not allowed to rest before and after being rolled out, which makes it lose its elasticity before being baked.

Why was the pastry hard and tough?

► The raw pastry was overmixed in the bowl or kneaded too much.

► Too much liquid was added to the blended-in flour and butter mixture.

► Too much flour was used for dusting the work surface when rolling out.

Why was the bottom of the tart soggy?

► The cooked pastry shell was not brushed with beaten egg white while still hot.

► The cooled pastry case was not brushed with a thin layer of apricot glaze before adding the filling.

CHOUX PASTRY

Why did the pastry collapse as soon as it was removed from the oven?

► The pastry was not baked long enough, it must be thoroughly crisp before removing from the oven.

► A hole was not pierced through the bottom of the cooked pastry. The trapped steam caused the pastry to soften.

► The oven temperature was too high.

MERINGUES

Why did the egg whites take so long to whisk?

► The egg whites were too cold. They must be at room temperature before whisking.

► The bowl or whisk was slightly greasy. They must both be spotlessly clean.

► The eggs were not fresh.

► A little of the egg yolk was dropped into the egg whites during separation. The fat in the yolk inhibited the egg whites from producing a good foam.

► The whites were not lifted up high during whisking. This helps to form a good airy structure.

Why did a clear syrup run out of the meringues during baking?

► Granulated sugar was used and did not dissolve fully. Try using superfine sugar.

► The sugar was added too quickly or too much at once so that it did not have time to dissolve.

► There might have been some form of moisture present in the oven during baking.

► The meringue was not baked immediately.

Why were the meringues still damp in the middle after baking?

► They were not baked and allowed to dry out in the oven long enough.

CREAMS, ICINGS, & FILLINGS

Why was it difficult to whip the cream into peaks?

► The cream, whisk, and bowl were not chilled well enough before use.

► The cream was not fresh.

► Sugar was added too early in the whipping process.

Why did the icing or whipped cream have lumps of confectioners' sugar in it?

► The confectioners' sugar was not sifted before it was added. Lumps of confectioners' sugar never disperse once they are mixed with other ingredients.

Templates

Use these templates to help you decorate the Teddy Bear Cake (see page 136 for the recipe). Carefully trace the teddy bear and the number appropriate to the age of the child onto a sheet of waxed paper or baking parchment. Then cut them out and use as described in the recipe.

Index

Acknowledgments

Author's Appreciation
I would like to thank the many people who have been involved in putting this book together. The team at Dorling Kindersley has worked long and hard over many months. I thank Debbie Major and Carolyn Ryden, my project editor and senior editor, for coping with my text; Jo Grey for her fine artwork and selective eye; Susannah Marriott, whose inspiration this book was; and Carole Ash, who had the vision. I enjoyed working with them all. It was good to see my recipes prepared so beautifully for photography by Janice Murfitt and Angela Kingsbury; and to work with Dave King, who took such wonderful photographs despite the highest summer temperatures imaginable. I wish to acknowledge with gratitude my good friends Lynda Dyer and Joanne Hill, who helped me prepare and test the many recipes, and Virginia Owen, who spent many long hours with me in my kitchen. I especially wish to thank Valerie Barrett for her support in working out recipe problems and exhaustive testing. I thank my friend Hans van den Klinkenberg, Swiss Chef Pâtissier, who allowed me to use two of his recipes. Lastly but not least I must acknowledge the various cooking writers from around the world in centuries past, whose books inspired me to write in the first instance.

Dorling Kindersley would like to thank Catherine Atkinson for preparing some of the cakes that appear in the book; Nasim Mawji, Claire Benson, and Jackie Jackson for editorial assistance; Vanessa Courtier for initial design work; Annette O'Sullivan and Kate L. Scott for design assistance; and Gilly Newman for illustrations.

Picture Credits: Key to pictures: t=top; c=center; b=bottom; l=left; r=right
Photography by Dave King except: Martin Cameron 30–1; 32–3, 34–5, 36–7, 38–9, 40–1; Terry McCormick 11, 13cr, 13br, 21, 75, 114, 128–9; Andy Crawford 41t, 145tr, 145cr, 145br; Steve Gorton 32tr, 32cr, 32br; The Bridgeman Art Library 6–7; Mary Evans Picture Library 8; The Hulton Deutsch Collection 6bl.

Mail Order Addresses for Baking Equipment and Supplies
The King Arthur Flour Baker's Catalogue, P.O. Box 876, Norwich, VT 05055; telephone (800) 827-6836
Williams-Sonoma, Mail Order Department, P.O. Box 7456, San Francisco, CA 94120; telephone (800) 541-2233
Wilton Industries, Inc., 2240 West 75th Street, Woodridge, IL 60517; telephone (708) 963-7100 ext. 320